Potter's Hand Poetry

Mary D. Wasson

Publishing

Published by Innovo Publishing LLC
www.innovopublishing.com
1-888-546-2111

Providing Full-Service Publishing Services for
Christian Authors, Artists & Organizations: Hardbacks, Paperbacks,
eBooks, Audiobooks, Music & Videos

Potter's Hand Poetry
Copyright © 2011 by Mary D. Wasson
All rights reserved.

Scripture taken from THE HOLY BIBLE, NEW INTERNATIONAL VERSION.
Copyright ©1973, 1978, 1984, by International Bible Society.
Used by permission of Zondervan Publishing House.

ISBN 13: 978-1-936076-45-1
ISBN 10: 1-936076-45-4

Cover Design & Interior Layout: Innovo Publishing LLC

Printed in the United States of America
U.S. Printing History

First Edition: May 2011

How it all started...

On December 16, 2009, for fun, I thought I would write a little quick poem to go along with some candy canes that I wanted to give my son's first-grade class at their Christmas party. I sat down at 9:00 p.m. that night and within ten minutes I had written this little poem. (The poem "Gift of Sharing" is in the seasonal poems in this book). My husband and I were both amazed how quickly the poem came, even though it was short and cute. I really never gave it a second thought at the time. God began a work in my life and I did not even know it. A month later, my almost twenty-year career in the consumer product goods industry began crumbling. Nothing had changed as far as my dedicated and excelling work ethic, so I was taken aback in shock. Later as I fought God, He made it very clear to me that this was going on company-wide and it helped, as I now did not take it so personally. It still hurt deep though. I was not ready to let my career go because I was in my comfort zone. After becoming physically, emotionally, and mentally drained from fighting God, I laid this at His feet. I knew He was closing the door on my career. At the very same time in early January, it was as if God literally picked up a jar of "writing potion" and poured it into my life. I began writing poetry daily and many times I would stop and cry because I was amazed with this new, beautiful gift of writing He had given to me. I felt so privileged and honored and I want this poetry to glorify God above all else.

I wanted a name for the poetry because I felt a book would soon follow. One Sunday morning in the shower, after I had been praying for several days on the name God would give this poetry, He revealed something in the shower to me. *Potter's Hand Poetry* came to me and I pondered, "What does this mean?" He spoke to me through the Holy Spirit and said, "I am the potter, Mary, and you are the clay." As I said all along, every poem comes from Him and I am just the vessel He is using to put it into writing. He is forming and shaping me into what he wants me to become, and I am so excited about fulfilling the purpose He has for my life. My deepest prayer through these poems is that someone will come to know Christ as their personal Savior. If this happens, and I know along the way it will, then the poems have served their purpose.

I have written about special people in my life to include my precious family and friends; children as they delight the soul; the Guatemala mission, because mission work is very important in my life; and encouraging poems to help people through so many walks of life. I hope you find many favorites that you can share with others who you love and care for each day. Before each section of the book, I will give you more insight on how some of these poems were created.

God gave me the majority of the titles for each poem during many of our quiet times together, and I would just stop and say, "This is a title for another poem, isn't it, God?" and thus, this book was created.

These first three poems say it all in "Breathed This Gift into Me," "Why Me?" and "Potter's Lesson."

I hope you laugh and I hope you cry as you savor each poem that the *Potter's Hand* has given.

The *clay* He is forming,

Mary

Table of Contents

Breathed This Gift into Me . . .
for My Father Above

At the beginning of this year, Dear God, You breathed this gift into me
And in my wildest dreams, I could not have picked
a more perfect gift to honor Thee

As each story is told through this beautiful gift of writing poetry
It reminds me over and over that you can use any gift given from above
to help others to see

I hope each poem will grasp hold of a heart
in a new way as the goodness of You is told
And I will give You all the glory
whether one or one thousand poetry books are sold

For You handpicked me only in Your perfect time
And I can use my gift of creativity and my love for You through each rhyme

It absolutely amazes me, and also others, how each one tells a beautiful story
Just enough lines to keep the interest and, of course, give You all the glory

I can write these poetry stories in fifteen to twenty minutes maximum
And people who strive to become poets could take days to finish some

This is proof that it only comes from my amazing Father
As through each one, many a heart You can stir

I have never taken a poetry class in all my days
And it makes me think of a potter forming his masterpiece of clay

It takes practice and more practice to get it right
But when You, the Almighty God, breathed life into it ~
any gift can be given overnight!

I know this poetry is giving me the confidence I need
As years ago in the Valley of Texas, You planted that seed

That one day we would write a book of my mom's life
For she suffered so much through all her strife

But we have the good news because with God ~ only He can get us through
For He promises in the Bible that He only wants His best for me and you

As I close this poem written to You, my dear Father
All I can say is, "I love You with every part of my heart and soul,
and I can't wait to take with You this new adventure."

"Your servant who thanks You for again breathing this gift into me
As I know You are right here with me,
for I feel You breathing so closely."

Why Me?

Did You give me such an incredible gift of writing poetry?
As I know this came from only Thee

In my days ahead, I feel so honored to be selected by You
To use these gifts and talents
And dedicate my life to only You

You always seem to amaze
As you set my heart ablaze

I hope the fire I have for You will be expressed through and through
A special twinkle in my eyes that is glowing from You

So in the days ahead
I will never say, "Why Me?"
Because I know, You will know why you chose ~ Mary . . .

Potter's Lesson

After the Potter perfectly forms His clay pot
It is gently placed on a shelf to wait, as this waiting period has this clay pot
wondering, "For what?"

It is not about waiting like we do impatiently in line at the store
No, it is about being still and getting even more connected with our Potter,
instead of feeling like we are being neglected or ignored

Sometimes in our daily lives, we feel our Potter has turned His back on us
And our clay pot becomes drier and drier because in Him, we lose our trust

We long to have the Potter's hands on our moist clay again
With an ignited spirit that tells us with Christ, "Yes, I can!"

We can become anything God wants us to become
But, we cannot spend our time comparing ourselves to all the other pots with
their various shapes and sizes for much bigger are some

This is when we give in to our insecurities,
which can turn to anger, jealousy, and hate
When in God's eyes, He still has His perfect plan for our lives,
if only we will keep our focus straight

See, this clay pot had to dry longer than some of the other pots on the shelf
For it is going to be decorated with rubies and gold and used for a king ~ only if
we had not concentrated on ourselves

Or it may have a more modest, but just as important, purpose, as this clay pot
will hold water which will be given to children dying from thirst
And this drying cycle on the shelf had to be complete to keep this clay pot
from cracking or even burst

Never allow any dry season of your life to keep you from knowing
that God has a purpose for you and me
Instead, allow the Potter to form His clay just perfectly
as you pray this prayer: "Father, help my clay pot to glorify Thee."

Mia Faith, Mary, Mark, and Ethan

CHILDREN'S POEMS

I had the opportunity to begin selling framed poems in a local shop in the town where I live. This inspired some sweet children's poems that I hope you will enjoy. Children are precious and they teach us so much. Their honesty and how they see the world has inspired many poems that I have written. My life is richly blessed with my children on earth, Ethan and Mia Faith. You will read more about them in the Special People section of this book. One of my favorite poems in this section is called "Freckles," which was inspired by my son, Ethan. Sometimes, he views things quite differently and it is simply beautiful and, in this case, it inspired this poem. May you embrace looking at the world through the eyes of a child.

Mary with daughter Mia Faith who inspired the poem, "Cuteness and Curls"

Mary with son Ethan who inspired the poem, "Freckles"

A Daddy's Dream

Could you have ever imagined two precious children like your very own?
God must have truly wanted you to harvest some seeds
that you had previously sown

Most dream to have one of each
For with boys and girls there are so many different life lessons to learn and teach

Each one definitely has their own unique personality
Boys rougher and meaner and then girls sensitive and sweeter
~ just how God wanted them to be

Some of the best life lessons around ~
"Do not sweat the small stuff" and "cherish the small things"
~ are two good ones to be found

Yes, do not sweat or get upset about small things for they are just that ~ small
For you could be living with a child with cancer, a rare disease,
a birth defect, or a tumor, which would all

Be almost unbearable for most daddies to ever face
So remember to keep the small things in their place

Do your best to cherish the things in life that seem very small
For in a child's eyes they are just the opposite ~ oh, so very tall

Like playing a board game with your children, dress up one day with your little
girl, or a little fishing adventure with your son
These are the ways that you will become the rarest of dads for in their little
hearts and minds you have won

The Greatest Dad Ever Award
And no money could ever afford

For once there was a dad who took his son on a fishing trip
A day from work that he took off for he never missed, but decided this day to skip

There were no fish biting this day so the father told all,
"This day was an absolute waste."
But when the son rekindled this day years and years later, he said this was the
best day ever without a moment of haste

Daddies sure have lots of responsibilities in being the bread winner, a good and
faithful husband, and doing their best to still be a good dad and father
But God knows this and if you will allow Him to help, He will teach you how to
be the best in all your roles through life's amazing adventure

I would have to think it must be a daddy's dream
To have your children fill your life with joy and dashes of huge compliments on
being the World's Greatest Dad, which only builds your self-esteem

Just like it must be our Father in heaven's dream as well
For us to constantly brag on Him and want the whole world to know about Him
as we constantly tell

Yes, a new perspective on what life is about
Not on another promotion, more money in the bank, or having a fun ride, but
now without any doubt

A new dream, yes, a daddy's dream about being a daddy and father
To be first a Godly husband and second a Godly daddy, so I can wear my
World's Greatest Dad badge with honor . . .

Happy Father's Day
From your wife, Mary

Baptism Blessing

Dear Lord, bless our precious children as we dedicate them this day to you
As we can never say thank you enough
for all the good things in our lives you do . . .

Through this baptism blessing, pour Your infinite love into their hearts
As each day these children wake
~ they will wake with thanksgiving from the start . . .

And when these children close their eyes at night
Because of this baptism blessing ~ they know in their precious lives,
everything with You by their side, Lord, will always be all right . . .

Building Blocks and Buses . . .

Little boys are like building blocks and buses, you see
As they grow too fast like building blocks stacked so perfectly

They are like speed racers going v–rroom everywhere they go
And much like a bus full of people, little boys chatter and get louder
as they follow their mommies in tow

God, thank You for our little boy that You gave to our family
And each time I see building blocks and buses
~ I will smile a little more gratefully . . .

Cute as a Button . . .

Our little boy is cute as a button as we believe all would agree
For he is so cuddly and fun to play with ~ our little blessing is a gift
from God, and we humbly thank Thee

We hope to give him a good home with lots and lots of love
Just like the love that only comes from above

Each day he brings more joy to our lives as he becomes cuter still
And we are so grateful because our cute-as-a-button boy was once a dream,
but now he is definitely real . . .

Cute as a Cupcake

Our little girl is cute as a cupcake
With yummy icing, a sprinkle of glitter, a piece of candy on top
~ yes, unique details that God did delicately make

She is sweet to watch as she plays with her dolls and wants to become
more and more like Mommy each day
And we thank God for our cute-as-a-cupcake little girl
and all her precious girly ways

She will blossom into a beautiful cake as she grows
And just remember, you, cute-as-a-cupcake girl, take our love with you
wherever your beautiful life goes

Cuteness and Curls . . .

Little girls at an early stage in life develop cuteness and curls just like
God wanted them to
For as we look into their eyes, we can see the beauty of God with intricate
details and a pure innocence through and through

Their cuteness and curls can melt away any stress in a day
As we enjoy their sweet smiles, their unique laugh, and even whether or
not their unruly curls gently find their way

God, help me cherish the little things in life like . . .
cuteness and curls
For her love is a love we can never get enough of
and no matter how old she becomes ~
she will always still be . . . our little girl

First Words . . .

When a child is only a few months old
We can hardly wait to hear their first words as if a child anticipating their
favorite story to be told

The first words like "Mama" or "Dada" ~ oh, which one will come first?
we constantly anticipate
For I must be this child's favorite from these first words they carefully make

As this child grows a little older into toddler years
We wait for the phrase, "I love you," which simply brings us to grateful tears

Months go by and years fly past
When to this child their most important day has come at last

When their first words are spoken as they say, "I do"
Joined together in marriage with a love so precious and so true

As we anticipate so many first words in life ~ God must too
As He wants us to become His child ~ more like Him and so radiant a view

As we share so many first words with Him through prayers and thanksgiving
And cherish all the first words in our lives,
for memories with God and with our family make life worth living . . .

Specifically for your precious little girl . . .

First Words . . .

When our little girl is only a few months old
We can hardly wait to hear her first words
like a child anticipating their favorite story to be told

The first words like "Mama" or "Dada" ~ oh, which one will come first?
we constantly anticipate
For I must be this child's favorite from these first words she will carefully make

As she grows a little older into toddler years
We wait for the phrase, "I love you," which simply brings us to grateful tears

Months go by and years fly past
When to our little girl her most important day has come at last

When her first words are spoken as she says, "I do"
Joined together in marriage with her love so precious and so true

As we anticipate so many first words in life ~ God must too
As He wants us to become His child ~ more like Him and so radiant a view

As we share so many first words with Him through prayers and thanksgiving
and cherish all the first words in our lives
For memories with God and with our family
make life worth living . . .

Freckles

My son asked, "Mommy, where is the little boy with the polka dots on his face?"
Awe . . . the innocence of a child you just want to embrace . . .

Or another time he asked, "Mommy, where is the little boy
with the pebbles on his face?"
The pure honesty and seeing through the eyes of a child
you just want to again embrace . . .

God made each of us so unique
With intricate details each one for us to keep . . .

Whether a mole, some freckles, or a blemish or two
He made no mistakes when He made me and you

Like a proud canvas on display
Such an array of beautiful shapes and colors with cute little freckles because He
wanted it this way . . .

Help me, Lord, to view the world
more through the eyes of a child in the days ahead
No matter how different some may be with complete acceptance and love instead

For this is how You want my life to lead
As an example of love in this world of need

Yes, so much need for more love, only the true love You can give
With a childlike anticipation of a new life I can live . . .

So, I thank You, God, for my six, seven, or even fifteen freckles You placed on me
Because it shows that You took just a little more time when You made ~
unique me!

Inspired by my son

Giddy for God

You know the feeling when you are young and you get giddy for someone
Many times referred to as puppy love when it is all said and done

Well, you can experience a greater kind of feeling
~ a feeling that will make you say, "Wow!"
When hearing the name, you perk up with a melting smile,
a fast-beating heart, and a lifted eyebrow

I am not talking about just any kind of giddy love
I am talking about the most perfect, complete,
and almost indescribable kind of love

A love you just can't quit talking about
For it is such an emotional and deep kind of love
you never want to live another day without

And as the days go by
You find yourself falling more in love with God
leaving you many times speechless with an emotional sigh
For He will become so evident in your life

*and you will never want to leave Him out
Of any and every mild or major decision,
for He will guide you with complete peace and never any doubt*

*You will miss any day that is left without quiet time you normally have
between you and Him
Going through your day like a little child struggling on their first day
as they learn how to swim*

*And you will feel like your day is helplessly getting behind from the very start
Because you didn't spend time with your most perfect love,
and now there is an ache deep inside your heart*

*Yes, it is being giddy for God and then giddy some more
For now you know your purpose in life
and cannot wait to see what your remaining journey has in store*

*There needs to be more people in this world becoming giddy
For only You, my God
~ yes, giddy with an eternity in heaven as their guarantee*

*And then in heaven together we can all be giddy one day
As we spend our eternity together in Your most perfected way . . .*

Having You for My Mommy . . .

*Having you for my mommy is the biggest blessing of all
And through the years as I grow, I hope to carefully each way recall*

*God must have thought I was a little more special in my own unique way
For He gave you to me, Mommy, as His masterpiece of clay*

*I knew you would be the best mommy ever to me
For you are a reflection of Grandma, who was the best mommy
you ever did know and definitely see . . .*

I Am Never Far Away

My dear son, I am never far away . . .
As Jesus allowed a part of my spirit to remain with you always

Good memories are something you will always have and will stay with you
Whenever you may feel scared, confused, when you are happy, or even blue

My love for you grows stronger each day
And now Jesus is allowing others to love you just as much, I pray

My son, you will do wonderful things one day
Because you never gave up and I was never far away

So whenever you want to talk to me
Jesus and I are listening and will help you be

Strong, loving, kind, funny, happy, and so much more as these are all
a reflection of Jesus living in you
And hopefully a reflection and fond memories of your mommy too

So, son, as you grow up and have your own family to love and hold
You can share great stories of you and me as they will forever be told

For I am never far away . . .
And Jesus, you, and I will all be together again one day . . .

For a child who lost his mother

One for Me, Two for You

I will only take one, and you have two
For sharing and generously giving is the right thing to do

The less time we spend thinking of me and only me
Is when we have more joy in our lives because we have opened our eyes to see

That acting like Jesus is expressed in the daily giving
that is so unnatural for us to know
And only with Christ living in us can we allow Him to show

One for Me, Two for You should be an unselfish characteristic that we desire most
In a humble way without ever taking time to boast

Therefore, in my days ahead I am so thankful that Christ is the One for Me . . .
And with Christ living through me, we can be Two for You . . .

Pretty as a Pink

My precious grandmother used to say, "You are as pretty as a pink"
As she smiled with a loving wink

Girls love the color pink when they are small
And as I grew up, I still love the color pink
because memories of Grandma I would recall

God gave us beautiful colors like pink to enjoy
And I am so thankful for precious sayings like: "Pretty as a Pink"
that bring me still today fond memories of complete love and joy . . .

Dedicated to Mandy and Niki's grandmother

Snow Day

How fun when we have a snow day . . .
A day where we can stay in our cozy homes and then go out and play

Play in this beautiful white as white snow
And make snowballs for each other to throw

Then lie down and make a snow angel
As if we are waving to heaven in a way to tell

Thanks to Jesus for allowing us to enjoy His beauty
Outside where we can feel so young and carefree

He wants us to enjoy time together with much laughter
His amazing wonders of nature like snow that is brrrrr . . .

So the next time you have a snow day
Don't forget to thank God as we pray

For this relaxing enjoyment that He brings
That makes our hearts feel young again and sings

And mostly for these memories that may
Bring us closer through God giving us this one . . . snow day

Some for You, Some for Me

Some for you, some for me . . .
When we learn about sharing then we have found that special key
Especially when we share Christ with others, you see
Because God requires this of you and me . . .

Some for you, some for me . . .
Go ahead; there is plenty to be had
So less and less people will feel so sad

Share a hug or a kiss so someone's heart will skip a beat
Showing this kind of extra love can be ~ oh so sweet

Some for you, some for me . . .
Would you like some of my candy?
Don't forget Kelsi, Dylan, Logan, Ethan, Mia Faith and oh, our friend, Mandy

Some for you, some for me . . .
There is just so much given to us
As God must have felt in us He could trust

And He gave some for you, some for me . . .

Yes, it is time to allow God's love to spread
Because He will be our bread

Bread of Life

So, some for you, some for me . . .
I am so glad He makes extra keys . . .

GUATEMALA MISSION AND MISSION WORK

This next section of poems holds some very special memories for me, inspired by many mission trips to Guatemala. Guatemala, Central America, is very dear to my heart because my mother was born and raised there in a very poor village. She has a beautiful testimony and moved to the United States when she met and married my American father. Her life was not the American dream. The only thing good that came from this marriage was my sister Melody and me. I am currently writing a book about her life story. Almost twenty years ago, God gave her a literal dream to begin a mission in the poor village where she was raised. She now, at the gentle age of seventy, travels back to Guatemala two times a year to do mission work. She has shown me and taught me how incredible it is to work full time for God. Whenever she talks about the Guatemala mission, she lights up like a Christmas tree because she is truly in her element. God gave me some special poems as I have traveled to do mission work. There are so many dedicated people in Guatemala who have fasted and prayed for my family and me through the years, even when they did not even know us. To be so many miles away and care so much is simply humbling to me. Also, many of these poems were given as a way of saying "thank you" to so many people who have donated items each year for us to take and give to very poor people who have nothing. I hope you will be touched by some of these mission poems and have the courage to step out in faith and fulfill your own mission God has in store for you. Take a "Vacation with Jesus" and see how He can, and will, change your life forever. It will be the most memorable vacation ever!

Mary's mother, Esperanza, who founded the Guatemala Mission Santa Fe

Guatemala Mission Santa Fe inspired the poem, "Guatemala Mission"

Making fun crafts at the mission with Guatemala families inspired the poem, "We are the Hands and Feet--You are the Body"

Guatemala Mission

It began with a dream God gave
For in the years ahead many souls would be saved
Just by His servant stepping out in faith
in what seemed impossible for most to believe
Yet this is how God works in ways we can't even conceive

19

Land was to be purchased in a very deserted place
As one day this mission would grow and would need the space

Most in the village thought and said, "Why would they want land way out here
Instead of having a mission in town with so much near?"

Yet God had the perfect place picked out way ahead
A place that would become Santa Fe Mission where many souls would tread

See God doesn't want it to be showy in the middle for all to see
As to say, "Look it is about me."

No, God wanted this mission to be in a very poor and almost remote part of town
Because one day it would be renowned

He slowly, through the years, allowed this mission to grow block by block
As He knew these children would become his flock

He did show out along the way through the beauty this church and mission bestows
So that each and every one who comes completely knows

This is how He will bless when we are faithful and true
Because unfortunately this consists of very few

Sister Esperanza has become the little Mother Theresa
in this poor little village abroad
As she comforts so many and invites them to this beautiful church
that was one day long ago just sod

She never gave up on her dream of seeing God turn block by block
this into a mission for missionaries to come
To help win souls for Christ one by one

To man it seemed an impossible task
But to God we just have to be willing to ask
He will take us places that today we can't imagine how great it could be
But with Him as our captain and lead it is only the best
for His children who believe

This mission will be a legacy that she will leave
As a reminder through great faith there is nothing we can't achieve

So many souls are rejoicing in heaven today
Because of her caring and dedication to help them find their way

As she begins her life in her seventies, this mission is still always top of mind
Because there are so many souls who still need to find

Find this amazing Heavenly Father who loves them so much
And in their heart feel His loving touch

And give their life to Christ and forever be changed
while spending time in heaven with Him forever
Just because His servant acted upon her dream
and knew He would come through and would never say "never"

We hope more and more missionaries have the opportunity here
to serve in Santa Fe
For you will never come home in the very same way

So many prayers have been answered and miracles come true
Because this is a true miracle of all that our God can do

So step out in faith and allow Him to take you places you have never been before
As you allow Him to shut some windows and open that one door

This one door opened could make a difference in this world
of people dying and going to hell
That is why God gives us the opportunity to lovingly share and tell

There will be a big celebration in heaven one day
From all the saved souls who found new life in Santa Fe

So allow your own miracle of a "Guatemala Mission"
to start from one planted seed
As we know this is a dying world of sinners who need

To know Jesus as their personal Savior and Friend
And spend eternity rejoicing with you and Him 'til the very end . . .

21

MARY D. WASSON

Sandals

*In poor countries of today, it almost seems you can tell the status of people
just by looking at their feet
Which would immediately make some appear in complete defeat*

*For many have soles as hard as a rock
Because they have never had the luxury of wearing shoes,
much less a choice of a certain color sock*

*They have been accustomed to the conditions in which they live
Just like we have become accustomed to the wealth
with a chance and a choice we can make to finally give*

*On a recent mission trip to Guatemala,
we had the opportunity to give new sandals because of a
Beautiful donation from friends who they may never meet
And as the new sandals were placed on each person's feet, we took their photo,
for the moment would not be fully complete*

*As photos were viewed, we enjoyed stories from our mission trip
And as we looked at these photos, our hearts would soon be gripped*

*For you could see in their eyes the importance each one felt
And in these moments as you personally witness this gift, your heart simply melts*

*As we think back for a moment to our own closets
with all the shoes from which to choose
We can get caught up in materialism ~ forgetting the poor around us,
for in our wealthy society we simply loose
I wonder what it would be like if we all had the same sandals to wear
Without elaborate heels, diamonds, colors, and name brands to compare*

*Just like in the days of Jesus with plain and simple sandals as we walk
Therefore; never allowing comparisons as we look down on others and talk*

*The next time we want to purchase some really expensive shoes ~
we should think of the cost
For in this very same price tag, so many souls for Christ could be won or lost*

Yes, today, many of us need this wake-up call
As we humbly thank Jesus for the reminder through sandals
and the sacrifice He made for us all

May we all make a sacrifice and give in a new way
So many poor people can feel a sense of self-worth through their new sandals
they proudly display

Yes, sandals for the young and old
As a new generation of stories in giving can be cherished and told . . .

We Are the Hands and Feet
~ You Are the Body

As our mission trip begins on a journey to Guatemala this June
Before we know it, we will look back and feel it ended too soon

We are the hands and feet God has selected to go
But you, church family, are the body who will remain
with loving support through unique ways will show

Every knee that has or will bow as you pray to God to bless this trip
And every encouraging word spoken in support that comes from your lips

For every sacrificial dollar you gave so one more good deed could be done
And, who knows, something even so small given in love
can return one more soul to Christ that was won

For every piece of fabric you became so excited to purchase
and could not decide which ones to get
Making the decision, "Well, I will get more than one
because of all the beautiful choices"
right here allowed God to let

You be a big part of this mission trip indeed
And, yes, plant several more God-blessed seeds

For a member who had a garage sale of her own one Saturday
And gave every dollar she made to the mission trip as her own creative way

For the couple who donated a case of Bibles in Spanish
So souls could come to know Christ in their own language

For the widow, after she heard recent testimony, listened to God as He said, "Give"
And now will be a big part of feeding the poor through bags of food given,
and for a hungry child another day he or she can live

Any and every time you stop and wonder what is taking place
Remember to voice a prayer of gratitude and praise and ask God to guide us
with His map He has traced

There are many reports of the weather
with enormous rain and tropical storms being so bad
But do not let this scare you, for God wants you, for us, to stay strong and not sad

Praising is contagious so praise Him every day for our mission trip
And we will feel it, my friend, and praise Him, too, in Guatemala
as each day He will fully equip

We are the Hands and Feet who will give gentle hugs, kisses, laughs, smiles,
praises, bagging food for the poor, visiting family after family in the village,
and having fun activities for the children

All with the desire of one more soul to save
You are the Body who God will bless each and every one
for your creative, unique, and supportive ways you gave

When we return, we will become the body again as we reunite
As God will send others out into the mission field, to the hospitals, nursing
homes, to the young, to the old, to the black, to the white, and out into the
community to ultimately be . . . His shining light!!!!!!

May We Shine Beautifully in Guatemala for Him . . .

Love ~ Ceta, Patsy, Mary, and other
missionaries serving Him

Fainting Love

In an evening in Guatemala where a young girl was recently healed
Became a completed moment in joy when her mother kneeled

Giving her life to Christ this very June 2010 night
For she had witnessed in the days before the miracle of her child's healing
with her very own sight

This young girl named Gladys became so overwhelmed with gratefulness
For God was giving her even more good things and not less

She broke down sobbing for over one hour
For God had rescued her and her family from death's tower

She was just praising God as she knelt with her hands, feet, and head to the floor
For this was just too much joy and thanksgiving
that she just could not take anymore

We walked her back to the missionary house in hopes of calming her
with a glass of water
As she was still sobbing in praise to the Heavenly Father who lovingly loves her
In an instant as I was rubbing her hair and hugging her with hopes to give comfort
is when a calm came over her and she lay back in faint
On the missionary house porch with so few around; therefore, quiet and quaint

I have never experienced anyone with fainting love
And this must have been what the Father wanted me to a be a witness of

A gratefulness and praise that I just cannot contain
As Your love, Father, pours down on me like glistening rain

Wow a fainting love for You Father above~
Was proven to me through this child who is giving You all her love

May my fainting love for You one day appear
As I open my eyes in Your presence, my Father so very dear . . .

Fabric ~ Act of Kindness

So many beautiful colors and textures of fabric are on display in fabric stores
Giving us fun and creative patterns and sewing tips and so much more

Would you ever think a piece of fabric given in love could change a life one day?
Well, God can use fabric as an act of kindness that can bring a new soul His way

As mission trips to Guatemala are made, pieces of fabric are taken,
as it is hard to take clothes to fit every size
And these fabrics can be used to make a beautiful blouse,
for God helps the giver, in giving,
to become a little more creative and wise

As a selection of fabrics are placed on a table for women to see
It is a twinkle of humbleness sprinkled with sincere gratefulness and a few tears
as you can see in her eyes as she thinks, "They care about me"

"Oh, which color should I choose, as I have never been given many choices in life
Instead, the only choices given to me have to do with more suffering and strife."
Thank you, Father, for the fabric ~ an act of kindness ~
you planted in my life to give
And may I think more of others each day as I live

So more choices sprinkled with hope and love can be sent their way
And this piece of fabric ~ an act of kindness ~ is a reminder to me
that, Father, You are the fabric of our lives today and every day . . .

Blessing of a Barbie

Most little girls in America have six, seven, ten, or, sadly, fifty, Barbies
with which they choose to play
Making it very, "Hard to choose only one favorite," you can hear them say

They are played with for a short time and then they become bored as can be
As frazzled hair and missing clothes at the end of their playing days
you can clearly see

They make it to the bottom of toy boxes or are stashed away
Or gladly sold in garage sales, for now they are bigger
and need more advanced toys to play

The Blessing of a Barbie is that she can be given a new home
with a child who longs to only have one
So all their love and attention can be given as this child becomes a playful child
having so much fun

My dream is that every little girl in Guatemala we meet can be given the
Blessing of a Barbie
As we find clothes through donations and sewing with love
and give Barbie a new life as little
Guatemalan girls play together in their homes of dirt floors
or in the streets so playfully

The Blessing of a Barbie is that they never grow old or wear out
Instead they can be given a new Barbie life where they can bring so much joy
with more hope and love steering away precious children
from hopelessness and lives full of doubt

Join us in bringing the Blessing of a Barbie
So we can together help God's children enjoy the life each child should have
with their very own Barbie, for they are so innocent and so precious
with love given so freely . . .

Vacation with Jesus

We are going on a vacation with Jesus; therefore, the preparation begins
Packing the right clothes and packing toys and anything that will allow us to
show the love of Christ so people we do not even know will let Jesus in

Yes, our vacation with Jesus can sometimes take us very far from home
But there are souls out there never hearing about this Jesus
as they casually and daily roam

Sacrifices are made to leave sometimes even small children behind
But Jesus sees all of this and is giving us an opportunity
that is truly one of a kind

*Just think of one more lost soul who will enter into heaven
and see Jesus' smiling face
Because you, my friend, let go of selfishness and luxuries
to help this lost soul win their life race*

*We put Jesus off and say, "I can't take that vacation with You this year
For all the things around me, like family and job, are just too dear."*

*If you want to go on the vacation of your life with Jesus called a mission trip
The promise is your life will never be the same because it was
from the same cup that Jesus sipped, you also sipped*

*And you became the only Jesus that some will ever know
Because of this amazing love of Jesus to each one you did show*

*Go ahead, my friend, and take this leap of faith
that will forever change your life ahead
And make this the best vacation ever
because you decided to take a vacation with Jesus, instead . . .*

Ethan and Mia Faith, who both inspired the poem, "Summer Days"

SEASONAL POEMS

These seasonal poems are really special as we enjoy our favorite season of Christmas. A few of my favorite poems that God gave me are called "Christmas Eve" and "Christmas Fragrance." They are beautiful reminders of the birth of Jesus and the free gift of salvation He has for you and me. I hope they become some of your favorites too.

The poem that I mentioned on how it all began is called "Gift of Sharing" that I wrote for my son's first-grade class. Another fun poem came along when he was in the second grade. I wrote a fun poem called "Santa's Message" that was read a week before his Christmas break. Then at his Christmas party, I read a poem that I had written where each child was mentioned in the poem in a cute and unique way. The children absolutely loved the poem and really believed Santa must have been watching them in the classroom for quite a while. I love when God gives me creativity for new ways to use the poems.

There is something beautiful about the different changing of seasons through the year. I hope you really enjoy another favorite, "Summer Days."

Gift of Sharing

It is Christmastime, it is Christmastime
We wanted to share these candy canes from our home to yours
In hopes that you may share some with brothers, sisters, moms, and dads
Because there is just so much to be had . . .

Sharing is a gift that comes from within
It is thinking of others this time of the year
That will continue to bring us good cheer . . .

So don't keep them only for you
So you can receive a Christmas blessing too . . .

For son Ethan's first-grade class

This House Believes

When the children are young, this house believes in Santa Claus
For make-believe is fun for children ~ yes, us all

As the children grow older, Santa Claus fades away
But the greatest One, Jesus, always in this house stays

This house believes in Jesus Christ every season of the year
And at Christmastime as we celebrate His birth,
He is even more precious and dear

Yes, this house believes and we want each guest to feel
As they spend time in our home, that He is truly real

This house becomes a home when Jesus remains the center in every room we go
For this house believes and our prayer is
when every guest leaves,
in Jesus Christ they will also believe and know . . .

Christmas Eve

The anticipated Christmas Eve has finally arrived today
As so many families gather together with loved ones as they rekindle busy
Christmas traffic, shopping stories, and sharing how another year
has almost gone away

With food galore and our favorite desserts
and Christmas presents underneath the tree
As we step back for a moment, we realize just how blessed we truly are,
for all our blessings we now with our loved ones around can clearly see

We play fun games which have become a tradition so everyone can join in
And then share family traditions we want to cherish with our dearly loved kin

The children just can't wait to see what cousins, aunts, uncles,
and Grandma and Grandpa bought

For just a week ago they were all in stores with a perfect gift with a discounted
price in mind they surely sought

Let us remember to anticipate the celebration of a precious Savior born
On that beautiful starlit sky known as Christmas morn

For Jesus came into this world to offer us a beautiful Christmas present
And this is our present from Almighty God for His one and only Son was sent

And all we have to do is receive Jesus into our hearts
Allowing Him to remain, in all we do, the most important part

And it doesn't matter about things like running a ten-mile marathon really fast
For see, many can't run at all, so this would not be a very fair task

Or if you and I could read the most books in a year
No, many in this world can't read;
therefore, this would not be fair to ask, my dear

My friend, there is nothing you can do to earn God's love, you see
For our good deeds are like filthy rags in His eyes because He wants us to accept
His free gift given just for you and me
All we have to do is simple ~ and that is just believe
And allow the wonder and magic of Christ's love to enter your heart through the
free gift of salvation given to you this Christmas Eve . . .

Christmas Fragrance

The fragrance of Christmas frequents our surroundings
as this blessed day grows near
Fragrances like live Christmas trees, hot apple cider, and, of course,
all the delicious pies that bring so much cheer

You can almost smell the fragrance of love as people become kindhearted
during this time of year
Listening to conversations about upcoming family gatherings because, for most,
being together is so precious and so dear

What if as the day grew closer to that Christmas morn
We could smell the beautiful aroma of a new baby right after He was born

This just might be the reminder we would all need
To remember what Christmas is truly about, instead of all the worldly greed

A true Christmas fragrance of the love of Jesus Christ who came
Into this world to save lives and with the good news to proclaim
That we can accept Him as our personal Savior
and our past sins will be erased, for they are one and the same

You will be given a new life with a new love that doesn't only come
at Christmastime, my friend
It is a love ~ a special kind of love that will dwell within you to the very end

You will transform into an image of Him with qualities that others long for
Like compassion, empathy, patience, perseverance, love, and oh so many more

In God's eyes the most beautiful fragrance anytime of the year
Is to have someone accept Him as their personal Savior
as He likely sheds an infinitive love tear

Yes, it all started way back with the Christmas fragrance
of true love that Christmas morn
The fragrance of this child named Jesus, who through His life gave us
the gift of a New Life reborn . . .

Christmas Lesson

The Christmastime has come again
when we all get caught up in the hustle and bustle
As we sift through the stores trying to find a perfect gift

We look for just a little thing that might bring a smile, a coo,
or a little happiness too . . .
We ask, "What will I get someone who already has a ton?" When the real
question should be, "Can people see Jesus in me?"

See, Jesus was born on that perfect Christmas morn,
this special day to give us a way, a light that should shine, One that is all mine,
so people will say, "They definitely found the way" and even if one day we go
astray, Jesus will still help them come back to Him

See it is not about a silly old tree or gifts shining with glee or about me, me, me
It is not about starting to pout because of a gift we did not receive

For see, we did receive the greatest gift of all ~ salvation to not only one, but
everyone who may call . . .
On Him to forgive them of their sin
For some Christmas day long, long ago, Jesus came into this world
as a way to show

And for us to know that He loves you and me and always wants us to be helping
others to believe so one day they, too, can receive . . . the greatest gift of all . . .
Jesus to live in their heart and always be a part of every decision that they make
and every childlike step we may take

Yes, this is what the Christmas season should be . . .
A time for the whole world to see ~ a Christmas filled with lots and lots
of Jesus in me . . .

Snowflakes and Santa

Dear Jesus, send snowflakes and Santa this Christmas to me
And I will leave you hot chocolate and cookies, just for Thee

Dear Jesus, I want to play in the snow and make a snow angel
As I wave to you in heaven and blow you a kiss to show you I am so thankful

Dear Jesus, You know what I want more than snowflakes and Santa though?
For others to have peace, joy, and love for when
we know You, Jesus, our lives will
peacefully, joyfully, and lovingly to others show . . .

Santa's Message

Listen, boys and girls, there is new talk on the street
That Santa has placed a secret video camera in classrooms all over the
world to watch children being naughty or really sweet

He wants this word of caution so every boy and girl will know
That Santa wants as much love and kindness to be given ~
yes, as much as you can show

Mrs. Kuykendall and Mrs. Cox and other teachers don't have eyes
in the back of their head to see if you are being good or bad
But no need to worry; Santa can see and is watching as he is
making his Christmas list and when you are bad, this makes Santa really sad

There is still time to turn things around
And when you are good, good back to you can be found
So do your best in school every day
And be good for each and every teacher along the way

And remember to say your prayers, too, at night
So Jesus, who sees all, will always help everything to turn out . . . just right

Easter This Year

Some may hear the word Easter and think of cute little bunnies, Easter egg
hunts, and maybe even a new dress for me . . .
This is exactly what retailers want for it to be

And nothing is wrong with special times with your family and friends
But stop for a moment in the midst of all this and ponder, "What will truly
matter in the end?"

How about admiring a dogwood in bloom as God seemed to delicately place these
for us to recall

That He paid the ultimate sacrifice for not a select few, but for ALL
So Easter this year can be our time to answer His call

And accept Christ as our personal Savior with a life never again the same
Having the Holy Spirit within us is far better than wealth or fame

We no longer go through this world alone just wandering around
Trying to find a purpose when one can never be found

But with Christ, He will reveal the exact purpose for our lives
and things will all make sense
With days filled with peace, joy, and hope and days less tense

For He promises, "I know the plans I have for you, plans to prosper you and not
to harm you, to give you hope and a future"
Jeremiah 29:11
And this is a promise from now on we can be sure

So how about Easter this year it become a new life in Christ you live
See, for God never promised, Easter next year to give . . .

With this poem "Easter This Year", I won my first local poetry contest and earned $50.

Summer Days

The joy of summer days
Riding bikes, having a picnic in the park, or a game of touch football to play

Summer leagues like t-ball or baseball
Fun for family and friends to gather all

Fun days of swimming for hours in the pool
Instead of studying for hours like we do in school

Taking a family vacation to the beach
"Are we there yet? Are we there yet?" the kids say because to them it is only
within an arm's reach

Watching fireworks on the Fourth of July
As we see all the beautiful colors and shapes as they touch the starlit sky

Having some watermelon as the juice drips down our face
And having fun with family and friends as we have a watermelon rolling race

Going barefoot for an entire day
For we have no special place to be or special clothes to wear
as we sure like it this way

Mowing the grass with Dad
For being with him can be some of the best memories we ever had

Sleeping in late
For getting up so early during school can be days we dread
or sometimes even hate
Getting up early to go to all the fun garage sales
As you brag to family and friends on all the bargains you found
as you share and tell

Sitting in front of a fan
As we sip some soda straight from the can

Going to Vacation Bible School
A really fun school as we learn about Jesus
and learn to follow the Living for Jesus rule

Getting a little part-time job to earn some cash
For money doesn't grow on trees and can be gone in a dash

Staying up late and watching videos or TV
For this is forbidden during school because we need our extra Z's

Going to the movies during the week with a friend
And hanging out together as we gladly give an ear to lend

Enjoying all the fresh fruits and vegetables like corn, tomatoes, okra, and peas
that come from our garden of love
As we thank Jesus for much-needed rain that comes from above

Oh, the joy of Summer Days
And I thank you, Jesus, for your season of summer shining down on us through
your beautiful sunshine with all your golden rays . . .

Awake to Autumn

The beginning of the crisp, cool air as you awake to Autumn
As this anticipated season has finally come

The changing of leaves bring the most magnificent colors of splendor
Each one painted in the boldness of colors so bright and beautiful,
yet so delicate and tender
Autumn seems to have the smell of college and professional football in the air
As many football fans get ready to spend time in their favorite comfortable chair

Days of mowing grass finally comes to an end
Replaced with raking leaves as the stronger winds many does send

Wearing long sleeves and pants again with boots that are in style
And all the fall colors to wear is a nice change for awhile

Eating warmer foods like soup, chili, or red beans and rice when you dine
Is warm to the soul and definitely the stomach and will do just fine

Turning off air conditioners and just using a ceiling fan when you sleep
Are evenings we would like to last for a while and even keep

Fall festivals are fun times for family and friends to enjoy
For the young and elder, moms and dads, for every girl and boy

The bright orange pumpkins get everyone in the fall spirit
As carving pumpkins are great moments with family as each fun face made is lit

The trick or treating and church festivals are a fun time together at Halloween
As we eat lots of candy and cute creative costumes are worn to be enjoyed and seen

So many wonderful memories are cherished from this special season as we
awake to Autumn~ yes, now it is fall
Thank You, Lord, for Your autumn season that through Your array of beautiful
colors You give to us all and cherished memories for many years
that we can warmly recall . . .

Magic of Love

We can hardly wait for the wonderful holidays like Valentine's Day or
Christmas to share the magic of love
Or birthdays and anniversaries that we also love to take notice of

The wonderful thing is that love can be a part of who we are daily
With no special recipe or any sort of magic,
for it doesn't have to be given just perfectly

A little bit of love can go a long way
Just by being courteous, offering a smile, opening a door, or being a good listener
~ all showing love without a word that we even needed to say

The true magic of love happens when you fall so in love with Jesus Christ
and transform
Into His child who wants to be just like their Father
and not to this world conform

The magic of love turns you into a person pleasing in His eyes
For love is and is not so many wonderful things like: love is patient, love is kind,
love does not envy, love is not self-seeking, love is not easily angered and love
brings proud people down to size

The magic of love is that "love never fails"
For in God's Holy Word in 1 Corinthians 13:4–8, He speaks of love, for in these
beautiful scriptures, He does lovingly tell . . .

SPECIAL PEOPLE IN MY LIFE FOR WHOM GOD INSPIRED A POEM

These had to be the easiest poems to write. To have the ability to write a poem about those you love or who have touched your life in special ways is such a blessing that I can't put into words.

The most important people in my life are my family and I have been given the privilege to write about all of them in one way or another. In addition, I am so blessed to have another family with my church family at First Baptist Nesbit in Nesbit, MS. What a blessing all of you have been!

You will learn more about me through the poems about my children, Ethan and Mia Faith.

I write about my mom—my absolute role model and hero—;my husband and our down-to-earth life together; my sister, who has always pushed me to do more because she believes in me; my niece, Kelsi, who God used to help me realize that I always wanted to remain close to my family when I lived far away; and my twin nephews, Dylan and Logan, who are too adorable and of course, who my brother-in-law Dennis would say, they take after him in every way.

There are poems on my wonderful in-laws, Gail and Carlos. The creative mind that God has given Mrs. Gail is simply breathtaking. Thank you for all the beautiful things your hands have made to bring joy to other lives.

I have written poems on friends and children. I wrote a poem "China Girl" for friends who were adopting a beautiful little girl, Emily, from China. I wrote "Three for Me," as many people in Guatemala fasted and prayed for a special blessing for friends, Nick and Kristy, not realizing the special blessing would be triplets! "Magnify My Memory" is a favorite poem on a friend who lost a loved one too soon. "A Day at the Farm" is a poem on the relaxation of taking a "farm day" with Papa Burt, my love-related papa. "The Storm Will Pass" was first written for a family I have never met who lost everything in the Nashville floods in April 2010. Later, God allowed this same poem for a special church family, Willie and Sarah, who lost everything in a house fire. "I Thought of You Today" was written in honor of my stepdad, Monk, who is in heaven now, and was the best father anyone could have ever had. I have also written several poems on those who I may have never met when the poem was written, but they inspired my life in such a special way that I knew God wanted their story to be told through this beautiful gift of poetry.

"Building Friendships Forever" is a special poem because God allowed me to start this new ministry at church, as we build friendships by being a friend. This means checking on the elderly and going by for a visit like we used to do all the time back in the past. We have gotten away from this and there are people who desperately need a friend.

May you receive a blessing from many people who have touched my life in such unique and wonderful ways.

Mary with her mom, Esperanza, who inspired the poem, "My Mom So Great"

My Mom So Great

My Mom So Great . . .
I know we were not joined together by mere fate

But God had a plan for you and me
So we could together in mission work help the world to see
This incredible gift of salvation that He gives us for free

We are not just daughter and mother
Even though I would never select another
See, we are each other's best friend
And always will be to the end

This gift of helping others that you show
And helping your grandchildren to know
Will be a legacy I, too, hope I can leave
So one day when they have their own children to conceive
They can see how to help others to believe

They will have learned how to love one another
And care not only for themselves, but for their brother
Because it started back years ago with their precious great-grandmother

She had a special gift indeed, helping others to succeed
As she helped so many believe
That with Christ, there is nothing you can't achieve

It started with a huge dream those precious years ago
As God used her in a mighty way to show
The people of Guatemala just how to know
This incredible Father above, not below

See, He used her because she was one of their own
And she could understand through the trials she had known
Through a simple act of love she has shown

41

To witness with compassion and love, this is what she is definitely made of
That is a gift very rare to find
Making this humble woman one of a kind

Yes, this will be her most important trait
And this is why she is . . .
My Mom So Great

Written by your daughter, Mary

My Husband, My Friend

My husband, my friend
And I hope we always will be to the end

You are just starting to fit like a good, comfortable shoe
It was as if God bonded us together with glue

We are still learning new things about each other as another year unfolds
And it is exciting and fun to see what that beholds

Some of our favorite past times may be quite boring to another
But I would never want to do them with any other

Like going to the latest movie
And having the movie theatre buttery popcorn until we could pop, pop, pop
But somehow, between you and me, we manage to finish every last drop
These are the memories I hope never stop

Or being in a hurry and grabbing some Krystal burgers
No, not the most romantic of dates
But at least we are not under a bunch of stress
Because we are trying so hard to impress

The simple things in life is what we will remember most
And in the years ahead, I will forever boast

From me going through my clean streaks
To you just being a down-right neat freak

Some may even say, "They have their childlike ways"
Like loving Scooby Doo shows just the same
And recalling everyone by name

For being a father to our kids
Showing them discipline and love
And showing them what a real father is made of
What more can I really say, except
"Thank you Father above because You are using us to show them
what life consists of"

I thank you for your encouragement and support
As these new ministries begin
Knowing if Christ is in the center of all of them, they are sure to win

Win other souls for Him
Because one day He, too, could use them

So hopefully this new gift God has given me of writing
Will continue to be very inviting

As I try to make other people's day
And having you right beside me along the way

Is just the inspiration that I need
So as a couple together in our loving relationship can succeed

God must have known what He was doing
When He hand selected you for me
And I want all the world to see

How blessed I am
Because God sent you to be
Just another extension of me . . .

My Husband, My Friend
Your wife to the end . . .

**Mary and Mark's son Ethan, who inspired poems,
"Ethan Grant" and "My Two"**

Ethan Grant

This child God Granted to me . . .
As I thought, this pregnancy was just so easy

Oh how shallow
But I would later know

Having my son was a dream come true
As I felt when I first held you

As the months and years passed by
I didn't realize how much I would ask why

See, some areas of your development seemed a little delayed
God used your aunt Melody to help me in a gentle way
realize on that terrible day . . .

That, yes, you indeed had mild autism
Immediately, I feared, "What about all the criticism?"

Oh what will this child have to endure?
As he was so young and so pure

We used all the resources we had
And, yes, having days where we just felt so sad

But we would do all that we could do
To give the best life for you

One night in months ahead
As you lie asleep in your little bed

Grandma, Aunt Mel, and I lay hands on you
Because there is nothing our Great God can't do

And we know what His word did say
About healing and taking sickness away
So we lifted you up to God as we prayed

Well as the months passed along
Our house began to sing a new song

Praising God for the new words you knew
And for the beautiful pictures you drew

Many days I just stop in awe
As I quickly recall

Of that very night that God began to heal
Just because we took the time to kneel

No, I do not take any of your
accomplishments for granted
Because little did I know your name would
mean so much
As such ~ Ethan Grant

Yes, God did Grant you to me
And through the trials I now see

Just how unique He created you to be
My son, you will always be my "boogie"

And my heart will always melt when
I hear you say, "Mommie . . ."

Written by your mom,
Mary

Mary and Mark's daughter, Mia Faith, who inspired poems, "Mia Faith" and "Priceless Moments"

Mia Faith

Well, it began on April 24, 2008
Having quiet time with God this Thursday morn'
Little did I know from this a child would be born

During this time, God so clearly spoke to me
As the Holy Spirit breathed life in me and said, "What might you ask?"
As I broke down I shared how I only wanted His will on having
another child as it seemed an impossible task

See after suffering three miscarriages in three consecutive years
Gosh, did I shed so many tears

I was so tired of trying this on my own
Because what I thought should happen was something I had not known
If only I would have let God shown

Then God spoke again and said, "Just ask Me your request
For My children, I only give the best."

I felt just like Hannah in the Bible as she prayed for this child she had longed for
This must have been what God had in store

So my prayer went something like this:
God, You know my every thought and wish and exactly what is in my heart,
but I sure would love a happy and healthy little girl to hold and kiss

Immediately a complete peace fell over me
As I handed God this perfect plea

It was as if He said, "Done.
I will give you your daughter not a son."

One week later the news came
And from this day I was never the same

It was a beautiful pregnancy except for a scare
Oh, my gosh this just isn't fair

We rushed to the hospital on June 5, 2008
It seemed we had such a long wait

The not knowing if this baby was okay
I would have to wait and see what the ultrasound would say

During this time God spoke to me about trust
And said, "Mary, this is an absolute must."

Well, the baby was great and growing just fine
Another way God would abundantly shine

Not by coincidence, Dr. Kristin Miller came
This amazing woman of great faith called me by name

God used this amazing doctor with gentleness and grace
To encourage me right then, right here in this place

She and so many others gave me so much encouragement
And God removed all the discouragement

See this was a miracle child and she would need a special name
Not one without a special meaning or lame

God would put her name in our path
Because through His greatness He hath

Blessed my life in a way I can't explain
As I glorify Him and try less to complain

On December 22, 2008, our precious little girl arrived
God with us, we did survive
every scare and attack that Satan tried

God gave her the name Mia Faith, meaning My Faith
In Spanish "Mi Fe"
I think this is the exact way

God would always want us to remember
everyone here and in Guatemala who fasted and prayed
Because each and everyone played
an important part of this miracle given that April morn'
And God I will forever adorn . . .

My love for you
As you exactly knew . . .
My Faith, Yes Mia Faith

My Two

I feel so blessed to have My Two . . .
Our rough little boy, Ethan, who loves his Scooby Doo

Our new baby girl, Mia Faith, who is into everything
Carrying stuff about and then to us she brings

It is so sweet to see this brother and sister play
As Mia Faith follows Ethan all the way

We love our evenings when we simply spend time together
Playing games, hide-and-seek and chase, as these memories they will
one day cherish forever . . .

Having our completed family was worth the wait
As if this was our fate . . .

So God, thank You for My Two
Because through them I completely see . . . only You

**Mary's sister, Melody, with her husband, Dennis,
and their children, Dylan, Logan, and Kelsi, who inspired the poems,
"My Sister, Melody", "Kelsi Hope", and "My Twin"**

My Sister, Melody

*From the very beginning, you always pushed me to be my best
And find ways to stand out from all the rest*

*Many times, mainly due to fear, I would fight it tooth and nail
Because I was so afraid I might fail*

*Somehow you always believed in me
And you were determined to help me achieve
Not just sit around and simply be*

*By pushing me to step out of my comfort zone
Even though I was scared to death of the unknown*

*You were the key in helping me start my career at Hershey
And nineteen years later, who would have thought this scared young girl, would
turn into a mature saleswoman just because my sister believed in me*

For awhile we had to live apart
But this never meant you weren't always close in my heart

And when our precious Kelsi came, I made a vow
That someday, someway, somehow

I would be close to my family again and move back to Memphis
So I could be a part of my niece's life and have her right there to hold and kiss

Well, God granted me my wish to move from San Antonio back close to home
As from our roots we never far want to roam

Your family was such an important part of my special day
as I started a new life in marriage
As Dennis pushed the twins so cute down the aisle in that precious baby carriage

Then as God allowed me to have my own son
To have a child, no special days in life can compare, no none

After this time God allowed me to grow so much closer to Him
As I went through many chapters in my life that were so dark and grim

The old Mary worried so much that I would one day disappoint the ones I love
Because of the many weaknesses I consist of

Well, today, I have such a new confidence ~
a confidence that comes from only Him above
As through mistakes I constantly make there is nothing more amazing
than His forgiveness and love

I do not have to try to be perfect nor do everything right
Because all that truly matters is that I love Him with all my soul and might

From this He sends rewards to His children
Because He knows the places we have been

Like our miracle baby girl, Mia Faith, so beautiful, so girly,
and sometimes just a little mess
Gosh, when God shows up ~ He does truly bless!

You and I may not always see everything eye to eye
But with sisters we know we are there to support each other
and never question why

Others who are blessed to say they, too, have a sister
Know that with only her
The bond only grows stronger and stronger

As we enter new chapters in our journey together where it holds so many
uncovered amazing dreams
Of inventions, poetry, writing books, and living on a farm ~ wow, it just seems

The most thrilling times are in the days ahead
And with my sister as my support we will tread

Through more trials, tribulations, joys, and revelations
As we both keep God in the center of you and me . . .

And He will smile down from heaven and say:
"See Mary, I had it planned out this way. When during the difficult times you
thought I wasn't there, I allowed Melody to be an extension of Me and today,
yes, we both can proudly call her, My Sister, Melody."

Kelsi Hope

Over eleven years ago the first of the legacy came
Given to her this very special middle name

Named after your precious grandmother
Why would we even consider picking another?

You are turning into a beautiful young lady, you see
Who has dreams and passions to one day be

Famous and dancing somewhere in between
And you definitely have the talent as all of us have seen

You came from a family of dreamers and this is a good thing
Because God will turn desires of your heart into desires of His heart f
or you so you can bring

Glory and honor to Him through all your days
As long as your heart remains to stay with Him
never forgetting to pray every step of the way

See Hollywood and New York at first glance can seem so appealing
But there is much in these places that are deceitful and revealing

The only promise you can ever count on is from your Heavenly Father above
Because He will never get tired of showing you His love

We know one day, Kelsi, you will be famous whether a dancer, a singer, an
actress, or maybe them all
Then I hope you can always recall

Sacrifices your family made to get you one step closer to your dream
Because seeing you in the spotlight, you simply light up and beam

Many ways you have always wanted to be like your aunt Mary
And God sure did bless us both with great hair . . .
Well, if there is one thing I would want you to learn from me
Is falling in love with Jesus is the only key

The key that will unlock so many doors for you to enter in
Because now it isn't just about me, but about Him

So Hope because this is what your middle name states
And this is a true testimony of your traits

Stay humble, Sissy, in this amazing journey you will take
And our whole family will be there crying, clapping,
and cheering you as you make

Your thanks to God in heaven above
As you delight yourself in His love
Then a simple bow to the crowd in gentle humbleness
as they see what you are truly made of

And then to all your family a gentle nod
Because we all know that this came from only God . . .
I love you ~ Aunt Mary

Kelsi was the first grandchild to my parents. She is such a beautiful young lady physically, but what makes her even more beautiful is her beautiful heart. God has blessed her with many talents and we know he has a very special plan for her life. She and I hold a very special bond as she likes to be like her aunt Mary. We are similar in many ways and we both have long hair and receive many wonderful compliments about this, yet I remind Kelsi that the outward appearance is temporary and what is most important is our love for Christ and fulfilling the purpose He has for these delicate lives while on earth. I hope I stay your role model, Kelsi, as you see how in love I continue to fall with my beautiful Savior. I am striving to be more like Him each day.

My Twin

Dylan and Logan

Almost nine years ago
God to Dennis and Melody did bestow
A set of twins, yes, two identical boys you know

And from the start
We had many times we just could not tell them apart

Sometimes you just have to mention a name
Because they are just so much the same

But God did make them both unique
Like Dylan who dawns a cute mole on his cheek
And Logan can sometimes be a little shy and meek

They have and will always be the best friend to each other
Because they would never choose another brother

God will give them both their own special talent to use to glorify Him someday
And to God in thanks they will pray

Grandma foresees a missionary and a pastor
And this just may be the door
God opens for you evermore

All I do believe
Is God the day your mom did conceive

Bestowed upon you, my dear twins,
The humility and ability to win so many souls for Him

Just know, too, I feel so honored to be your aunt
And I can promise you will never hear me say, "I just can't."

See God will always show His favor for both of you
Because you would not be complete with just one of you

So feel privileged to have a twin
Because you can count on them to help you win

And with God by your side
It will be the most amazing ride . . .

Yes, God, and of course . . . My Twin

Even though you are identical, you are both very unique in many special ways and I know God has a special and wonderful plan for your lives. I am so proud to be your cool Aunt Mary

My Other Mother

Can't imagine a more fitting time to let you know what you really mean
Just like my own mother, with you I have clearly seen

How to love and love some more
As this is what aunts are really for

This amazing love you provide
Is a love you unselfishly give and never hide

You are there for us any time we call
And there is no request that is ever too tall

You effortlessly turn into my other mother
Whether it be for me or my older brother

You may be called an aunt to me
But you also hold the title my other mother so perfectly

So we want to wish you a Happy Mother's Day
Because for you, my other mother, deserve this day to say
How double blessed my life is today
For God blessed me with my other mother and
I would never have it any other way . . .

Priceless Moments

"Mommy, I do not like the raisins in my watermelon"
Oh, a priceless moment from my precious son

Or when my son says, "I like the food on my plate except for these little trees"
As he referred to the broccoli on his plate and I just want to thank Jesus for this
innocence as I, many days, fall to my knees

"Mommy, where is the little boy with the polka dots on his face?"
Another priceless moment in time as you just want to hug your child with a
warm, loving embrace

A moment when your eighteen-month-old daughter walks into the room modeling
your high-heel shoes
As she longs to be more like her mommy as she gives these little clues

Or when she picks up the phone and has her own "baby talk" conversation
As if she was already grown up and acts so mature without any hesitation

When she walks around looking for her brother as she calls,
"Bubba, Bubba" as if to say, "Where are you?"
Your heart melts for these priceless moments as she loves her big brother
and longs for him to be close too

When she lights up like a Christmas tree whenever she sees her grandma and
yells, "Gum Gum!"
For none can compare to "Gum, Gum" ~ for she is the best one

Getting up and acting silly together as you dance when music comes on
And singing like rock stars as we sing out of key to a fun, fabulous song

Walking every morning to the end of the road as you put your son on the school bus
As he is grinning from ear to ear when he gets to sit by the window and some
days you shed a few tears as you thank God that He has allowed you to be this
child's parent, for in Mark and me, He did trust

Going on our family vacation to the beach in the summer
As we enjoy fun in the sand and even dress up for beach pictures in hopes of a
Christmas card to capture

Doing nothing at all, but just being together as a family
God, I thank You from the bottom of my heart for Ethan and Mia Faith,
as you remind me how precious their innocence can be . . .

Oh, to see the world more through the eyes of a child as their priceless moments
I will forever cherish
And my thanks to You, Father, for my children, Ethan and Mia Faith ~
a granted wish . . .

Grandma Gail

What better time than your birthday and Valentine's 2010 to express how much
we love our grandma Gail . . .
To share with our friends and family ~ yes, we never fail

To let you know how much we enjoy each and every play date
When you become not only Grandma, but our fun playmate

To show you all the new things we learn and know
As we are so eager to share and show

And we can always count on you to keep us in style with a monogram
And have others say how blessed we are to have a grandma like you as we reply,
"Yes, I am."

Hopefully, we will pick up some of your creative traits
And make others feel a little extra special or even great
As we can share a special part of ourselves with someone along the way
Just the same way Grandma Gail does each and every day

In our prayers at night, we always thank God for you, Grandma Gail
And we hope we never forget to show the love we have for you as we forever tell

Grandpa Gives

Probably the best gift a grandpa gives
Is quality time spent with his grandchildren in the days he lives

Whether a big hug and a kiss, a cheerleader during all their accomplishments,
or sometimes just enjoying together-time watching Scooby Doo
These times being together is the best gift Grandpa gives
as you are giving the best of you

You know the saying, "Grandchildren are God's reward for not
killing your children," which just may hold true
For being with your grandchildren, you can see a reflection of your own child
and they keep families together too

Sometimes when your children were younger
You could not be around as much due to providing for your family
while striving to be a better father

Well, God sees all this and rewards you
with the precious grandchildren He has given
For you, Grandpa, to enjoy as they sure make life worth living

So may we never take you for granted, Grandpa
For in our eyes, the way our Grandpa Gives surpasses them all . . .

Patsy, My Missionary Friend

I hope through the words of this poem you can clearly see
Just how much you mean to Mama, the people of Guatemala, and me

It started so many years ago
When you dedicated yourself to mission work
so others in Guatemala would know

About God's gift in giving His only Son
To save us from our sins because He is the only One

God so delicately orchestrated the bond that would develop
between Mama and you
Because He knew together the love you have for others would shine through

As you dedicate your life to mission work and plant one more seed
Because this world is in such desperate need

To find hope and a true love that will last and they can embrace
Because with God by their side they can finish their race

Not only did you commit to mission work in Guatemala
But so did Bobby, your precious husband, who gave so much love to them
And now he is in heaven rejoicing with the angels and our Savior ~ yes, HIM

Patsy, along the way Satan tried to attack
But you did not give up and each time you fought back

And today God has given you such a beautiful testimony to share
As you love each and everyone in Guatemala a
s you show them how deep you care

Patsy, my missionary friend
I know this mission work will continue with Mama and you 'til the very end

The end of your days here . . .
But your amazing journey will just begin
As you enter with Jesus to heaven within
He has a special mansion in store for Bobby and you
Because no matter the obstacles, you remained faithful and true

What a privilege to know you as you have persevered every day
And what a blessing to know you have helped so many find the true way

Yes, Patsy my missionary friend
You have helped the people of Guatemala many broken hearts to mend

And each time God has to look down from heaven and say,
"Patsy, I am so proud you turned out this way and I no longer call you a servant,
but I call you friend, and we will always will be to the very end . . ."
John: 15: 14–16

Patsy, you have been my mom's dear friend and missionary partner for many
years. I hope you know God is preparing a beautiful mansion for Bobby and
you to enjoy in heaven. Thank you for your dedication to the Guatemala
mission. Love, Mary

Our Fifty Years Together

It started way back in the fifties at Southside High School
Remember back to this age when we acted so grown up and so cool

God knew the very day He joined this young lady and this young man
That together for the next fifty years their life would span

They were high school sweethearts
Who rarely spent their time apart

Then on January 23, 1960, their wedding day came
And despite Satan's attempts, as Mildred had the flu,
this bond began one in the same

Then as their love grew so did their family too
On February 9, 1961, to them a beautiful daughter, Lesliane, was born named
after her father and her mother
Leslie and Mildred Ann knew because of the love and joy she brought that one
day God would send them another

To this very day, she resembles them both
And it is a simple reminder of their amazing love and their oath

Well, during this time they lived in California as Leslie was in the air force
They were here a little over three years as God was planning out their course

Well, we all know that from our true home
We never far, or at least for very long, want to roam

So God brought them home to Memphis and now in the country of Nesbit where
He settled them
And for this move they completely praised Him

A few years later the news came that a new sibling to Lesliane would come
Because blessings of a new child ~ we all know who this comes from . . .

On April 18, 1967, Leslie so proudly held Clint, his perfect son
And looked to heaven this day and prayed,
"Thank You, God, for all that You have done."

This family is now complete
As we now chase around this new baby boy
when we hear the pitter patter of his little feet

The years went by and their children grew
But this family as God in the center of them always knew

Their legacy would continue as they celebrated their amazing grandchildren one
by one with talents of their own
This has to be God's reward because through them His love is shown

We get to be childlike again as we celebrate Rachel, Christopher, Jacob, Daniel,
Garrett, and Madison
WOW, what an amazing gift You have given us, God, just like when you gave
your one and only Son . . .

Whether Leslie rides his tractor, helps widows with their yard work,
serves as a deacon, or goes hunting for a day
And Mildred paints a beautiful new painting, sews a new seam, or teaches
Sunday school . . .
~ their love is like a fresh bouquet

As we look back on our fifty years together, all we can really say:
"I completely praise You, God, that You had it orchestrated this way."

"For the next fifty years I anticipate
What an amazing journey it will be with you, my God-chosen perfect mate."

Dedicated and written for dear friends,
Leslie and Mildred

My Florence ~ Sent to Me

Through a newspaper article we met
Then through an evening at Olive Garden was set

The beginning of a new friendship we began
Because together as God at the center of our lives we can
Build on our bond that was not joined by man

But this special encounter that God had for you and me
Is just another testimony of how great a God He can be

It is as if we have been best friends for years
As we immediately shared our hopes and fears
And even shed a few beautiful tears

See, Florence, you were sent to me
All because of only He

And for this I truly adore
This friendship that will continue to bloom even more

I thank God for the encouragement you bring
Which is not just an unnoticeable thing

See Florence, God sent you to me
Because together through prayer we will be
An inspiration for others to see
Thank You, God, for My Florence ~ Sent to Me............

Florence and I met through a newspaper article and she holds a special place in my heart

My Dear Mrs. Shirley

You will always be My Dear Mrs. Shirley . . .
With your beautiful ocean-like blue eyes and silky pearl-like hair,
holding such a special place to me

God put you and me together many years ago
Because we both have such a love for Him and this He did truly know

It started because of your amazing ability to beautifully sew
And everyone who knows me knows this is not something to me God did bestow

When I look at all the beautiful curtains and pillows you have sewn
I think, What an incredible talent of sewing God has given you
It is a true reminder to me that when we are faithful and true

He doesn't want to give us talents any less
Than His absolute best

I will forever be grateful for your encouragement and prayer
as we awaited our miracle child
Because this miracle was a testament of our faith, which is strong,
not at all mild

God knew that one day I would need you to be
This encouragement and prayer warrior for me

Hopefully, through these heartfelt words I can somehow express
You entered my life to completely bless

As God has given me this new gift of writing
This has become so amazing and exciting

I hope as you celebrate another birthday this year
Through these words you can truly hear

Hear God say, "My dear Shirley . . .
You have used the talents I have given you to glorify Me and I have special
rewards in heaven just for you when you are here with me."

So I hope you can cherish these words given from Him to me to you and just know like you have been to me
I hope to others you can also be . . .

Their dear Mrs. Shirley . . .

Mrs. Shirley always reminded me to stay strong in my faith as God would send us another child in due time. I am inspired by her love for God. God has truly blessed her with a gift of sewing, and my house has some of the most beautiful curtains and pillows because each piece was sewn with love by my dear Mrs. Shirley.

My Pastor

What a blessing, my pastor
With him there is always an open door
To encourage us more and more
Knowing to love everyone every day can be a quite a challenging chore
But one day together we will celebrate on that celestial shore

God made him human just like you and me
With a little extra gift to help others to see
The only way to heaven is to accept
Christ as our personal Savior and ONLY He

Brother Gary was also blessed with another gift
Helping him make an easy shift

From pastor to singer all in one
Because his work is never done
Helping others to believe in God's only Son

I thank God for placing him in my family's life
To celebrate with us our joys and help us with unfortunate strife

But mostly for the friendship we have had the honor to receive
And the encouragement given and helping us to believe
Through prayer and support and with Christ as the lead,
there is nothing we can't achieve

His humbleness is a true reflection of the man most would want to be . . .
God has to look down from heaven and say,
"He is becoming more and more like Me."

Who knows what this new year will hold;
however, we do know that God had a special mold
One where you profess His love so strong and so bold

He has so many wonderful things in store
For Brother Gary, my pastor . . .

I thank God for you, Brother Gary, my friend, and my pastor.

Ann ~ So Gracious Indeed

My dear Ann as you celebrate another year
Only fond memories are rekindled making you feel less far, but rather near

You have truly been the best friend my mother, Esperanza, has ever known
Through the loving way Don, you, and your family took her and her two
daughters in and showered them with love like they had never been shown

Now all these years later, soon her story in a book will be told
And the first pages will be dedicated to you, my dear Ann,
with dreams for you to soon hold

You indeed are a rare and valuable mold of people in this world today
For you had your own family, yet Don and you chose
to help this poor lady find her way

Due to the language barrier, you displayed more and more love, which is the
universal language, for sometimes very few words of English or Spanish
could either of you say

And God built a beautiful friendship
and you became Esperanza's red-haired sister
Very rare in Guatemala, a unique and wonderful red-haired sister
~ thankfully, He chose to give her

Seasons changed and our family moved away
When I know in your heart you longed for us to stay

Times became hard again, but now Mama knew
this Jesus she saw so much in you
Because little did she know, you constantly prayed for her salvation
giving her life anew

She met and married an incredible man named Monk with gentleness and grace
Displaying so many of the qualities her sister Ann portrayed
~ an incredible husband and father became her dream come true
due to all she had previously had to face

Then God in the years that had past
Gave Esperanza a literal dream of His purpose for her life at last

And it was to go back to Guatemala where she grew up
and start a mission to help the very poor
And show through this same kind of love she learned from you
that Jesus was the open door

My dear Ann, your name means ~ One who is so gracious
With your gorgeous red hair ~ full of life and love ~ quite vivacious

You were introduced into all of our lives
And God used you with all your love to introduce us to Him
when you could have used the excuse
to only concentrate on your own family of five

You are a role model of what true friendship is all about
For sometimes it is difficult and not always easy, but making the sacrifice,
determining to release any doubt

Ann, you are so gracious indeed
And I have learned from you about planting a true-friendship seed

And Jesus now says to you, "I no longer call you servant,
but I now call you Friend" John 15:15.
"And my promise to you, my dear Ann, so gracious indeed,
is that this friendship will never end."

Ann, Don, Uncle Dan, and your entire family were who God used most to help our family in time of great need. They rescued my mom from a very abusive husband—my father—and never worried that they had become too involved. We can never thank them enough for all they have done for us and God used each of them to plant seeds of His amazing love into our lives. Thanks can never be enough for your family, but God has great things He is preparing for you in eternity. Ann and Don dedicated their home many years ago to be used to glorify God. Her family gives God all the glory and Him alone!

My Papa Burt

As this New Year begins, and this world continues to spin
It is always nice to know that love remains with us kin

We may not be blood related,
but we are definitely love related

God placed you in my life those many years ago
So through these years our love still continues to grow

We share special memories that only mean the world to you and me
These will remain in my heart
And you will always be my Papa Burt to me . . .

Expressions of Love
Through Pecan Pies and Turnip Greens . . .

People have different ways of expressing love to others
And yours, Mrs. Flo, is cooking,
which can sometimes be even better than my mother's

Yes, an unexpected, but welcoming call comes when you say,
"I made a homemade pecan pie that I wanted to bring your way."

My taste buds begin to water over the phone as I feel so blessed
To be the recipient of a gift God has given you, for if I tried to make a pecan pie,
it would surely be a mess

When autumn comes around
Healthy delicious turnip greens in some gardens can be found

This is when Papa goes to the farm and with love he gently picks
The most beautiful turnip greens and carefully washes them over and over ~
taking all day, for this is a process anything but quick

Then Mrs. Flo slow cooks them using her secret recipe sprinkled
with just the right amount of love
And, of course, she makes a batch of homemade cornbread, for every great meal
of turnip greens cannot be complete without some

God has given each of us our own expression of love to share
Each so unique as the individual He has given the gift to,
and unfortunately in today's households cooking is quite rare
Yet, Mrs. Flo, you show your beautiful and unique gift
given to you through your delicious Southern cooking
which shows others, like me, how much you love and care . . .

A Day at the Farm

A special day I will always hold in my heart is when Papa Burt and I
can take a beautiful day in spring
To head on down to the farm and enjoy the countryside
and all the beauty God brings . . .

We have to make a few stops along the way like our stop in Batesville
to pick up our bait so we can fish and stopping by also to say
Hello to my newfound friend, Jimmy,
who seeing me for a short spell seems to make his day

Then we stop at the Quik Stop for a soda and something fried to eat
like some sort of cheese taco
But, of course, the day I go in they are completely out so they must be really good
as the locals must know

We make another stop to get a dozen or two of fresh country eggs
My goodness, Papa Burt must think, I hope this girl doesn't make me stop again
and this will be our last stop I beg

We make it to the farm where lies on a small little hill, a mint green country
home with the dream porch for all to relax and unwind
Not many out there like this I bet with this wrap-around porch
~ truly one of a kind

Of course, this porch wouldn't be complete without the numerous hanging swings
And immediately when you sit on one you think of Uncle Herman
and all the beautiful memories he brings

At the most perfect time a gentle breeze seems to appear
As if Uncle Herman is making us feel comfortable
and welcoming us with his presence so near

I have to believe this is exactly what Uncle Herman would want it to become
Where laughter, rekindling great stories, relaxation, and good company comes

For in the country the simple ways of life are adored
And in today's hectic world, we definitely need this so much more

After Papa Burt checks on the house and we take a bathroom break
We get our fishing poles, get in the red truck, and head on over
to the most magnificent lake

Thelbert and William have been blessed with this beautiful land
and a picturesque lake
One where you can appreciate God's beauty and we couldn't pick a more perfect
place to take a break

Conversations in spring center around each and everyone's garden
Or updating us on the status of people in the country and their kin

See, conversations in the city revolve around finishing the next report
And more and more stressful topics about lawsuits
and who is taking who to court

What happened to these good 'ol days when someone needed a loan and you
knew they would pay you back by their word
Instead of today where we get it in writing
and make sure many other people heard

Yes, spending the day at the farm helps me cherish the simplicity of life and focus
on what "country roots" are all about
Where there is so much room NOT to rush to do anything
~ very rare these days no doubt

As we leave Enid, it just wouldn't be complete until we stop by the catfish place
for some great home-style cooking
As people spot Papa Burt and me, with I guess a city-like look, they are cordial
but I also catch them looking

It may not be as often as I would like it to be
But I sure do treasure a day at the farm, for I know it means much to Papa Burt
and "Papa, you know what, it also does to me . . ."

True Friend

A true friend in you can be found
And as I search near and far and all around

I realize this is a very rare thing today
As we do not take the time for others in this loving way

For we all seem to have so much on our plate
Yet God puts some friends in our path as if it were fate

Taking time to be a true friend is tested in their time of need
As in these times we have so many opportunities to plant a caring seed

See, people want to be your so-called true friend when you are riding high
But when you are knocked down these same so-called true friends
will just pass you by

A true, true friend will ask God to allow themselves to carry your sorrow
An expression of unselfishness for this day and if needed for tomorrow

For they do not think of themselves, but instead set an example
of what a true friend should be
And I am sure blessed that God gave your friendship to me
And I also pray that what I have learned from you I can also strive to be

For being a true friend is just this ~ being true
And I believe today we can agree this consists of very few

I am blessed to call you true friend
And God showed a little more favor when into my life He did send

You ~ so humble and rare
Helping in times when life seems so unfair

Thank you again for, yes, I am blessed to call you true friend
And I hope as the days pass I can be the same true friend on my end

For in this life we live we can always count on one true friend
and that is our Father above
And then to have another on this earth is an extra blessing
that He gave to us out of pure love

So Father help me to be the best true friend to someone
As my way of thanking You for all You have done

And I thank You, Father, for my true friend, Dave
For I know a special place in heaven for him You will save . . .

Building Friendships Forever
BFF Ministry

I thank You, God, last summer for giving me this dream
Of beginning a new ministry, which to me would seem

A much-needed love for one another that we sometimes forget
As the world consumes daily if we let

God even allowed it to have a cool name, BFF Ministry
Probably none out there quite like the same

Taking time for one another
And beginning to intimately know more about your brother

By just going by to have some lunch
And just having that simple ole visit that can mean so much

My how we have forgotten how to love like in the good old days of past
Because we allow life around us to move so fast

It is incredible when we can take time to smell the roses in a day
I really think God would want us to slow down this way

And truly build friendships forever
That will never crumble or sever

Because we invested our heart
These new friendships will always be a part

Of how I believe God intended it to be
We can be such a witness to others, you see

As they will say, "I can't believe you took time to love this way."

Yes, this ministry of building friendships forever
Could truly be unique in this New Year for all of us together

As we set our New Year's resolutions
Step out of your comfort zone as you will never go it alone

My friend, God will bless our new friendships we build
Whether young or old
Life has so much to be told

As we learn about he and she
God will remind us, it is not about only me

So as a church family as we sit upon this hill
Let us show the whole world that this is real

Let us be that shining light in the community
Which encourages a loving Christian unity

Yes, thank You, God, for this BFF Ministry
Because this just might be the key
Of just what You had in store for all of us, not only me

And who knows along the way, we may make one, two,
or how about six or even seven
And the angels will surely rejoice with our Amazing Father in heaven . . .

Mr. Jim ~ How I Came to Know Him

Mr. Jim and I met in Sunday school one day
As I was coming to encourage members to sign up
for the BFF Ministry coming their way

It is all about Building Friendships Forever . . .
So widows, lonely people, or the elderly will never

Feel as if no one cares anymore about them
For they should be important to you and me because they are to . . . Him

And God knew as He allowed a friendship to develop between Mr. Jim and me
That Mr. Jim was all alone as his precious wife
was now in a nursing home, you see

He has come to my house and met my precious family
And I have gone for some visits and had to go and get my homemade candy

So we do have something in common, as I am known as the candy lady
and he is known as the candy man . . .
Because he makes some of the best homemade candy like only he can

He was once one of the finest brick layers around
And still today could be one of the rare that can be found

Some days I know are harder for him
as he sees his wife going through this terrible disease
But just remember, Mr. Jim, to always ask God, "Help me, please."

And He will comfort you in a way like no other
Like a new baby being held so tight by his proud new mother

I thank you for all the encouragement and words of wisdom
As I learn more about God's plan for me
and hopefully along the way encourage some

Some lives in a positive way
Like building a new friendship that will always stay

Stay special because God orchestrated it all
And this is like our friendship, Mr. Jim, as we know on each other we can call

So, thank You, Lord, for Mr. Jim
Because, through You, is . . . How I Came to Know Him.

China Girl

Soon a new arrival is coming your way
And this will be the most perfect day . . .

The pitter patter of new footsteps
They may not be a baby's footsteps, but they will be
a child's footsteps that will enter your heart
and always be the most special part . . .

The bond that God will bring will make everyone's heart sing

As they lay eyes on God's perfect gift that He has given both of you
Just know your days ahead will be blissful and true
This China Girl God handpicked just like the baby so new

May we thank God for this incredible year
When this child will shed one less tear

For see, she will now have a family to know
As God selected her especially for them to show . . .
Faith, Hope, and Love
And the greatest of these is Love . . .

Dedicated to Mike and Teri as they
adopted daughter Emily from China

Three for Me

As we begin the year 2010, a new chapter in our lives,
a dream come true, a reach within . . .

May we reflect on the hardships we had to face and thank God for bringing us to
this special place . . .
An incredible gift ~ Three for Me
A she, a he, and another she

In the years to come they will bring more and more glee
And we will realize life is not just about me
This was God's gift that He gave us for free

We know God selected special people to endure these sleepless nights because in
the months ahead we know it will be all right

As we see a she, a he, and another she
We will ask, "God, how did I deserve these perfect Three?"

God will reply, "My child, you trusted and waited on Me. Just like the gift of
salvation is free for anyone who will believe in Me.
I knew Nick and Kristy this gift of Three would never be taken for granted as
you and I will see, this gift of Three will always be a part of you and Me."

Love–Related

We met one Sunday in church
As I allowed God to help me search

Another family I could come to know
And through simple acts of kindness hopefully show

That building a new friendship can be a blessing for them and me
As we allow God to let us see

That you do not have to be blood-related
Just willing to be love-related . . .

I will forever cherish our first visit when I brought Dale's lunch
And we visited and got to know one another as we sat around the kitchen table
talking a whole bunch

On one visit, Mr. Ray and I walked around the yard
As we looked long and hard

For some pecans to pick
Yes, these are memories that always stick

I have seen pictures of your precious family displayed throughout your home,
as I heard stories about everyone
And I could tell how proud you are of all that they have done

I have had the privilege of praying for Mrs. Sue
When sometimes she was in quite a deal of pain and probably feeling a little blue

I will never forget the evening after one of our prayers how she held me so tight
And I knew when I left she was one of God's children,
and He would see that she was all right

Like someone said, "When you make time for others,
God seems to stretch out the day."
I really believe this is the kind of life He wants us to display
And, yes, He will allow us time to find a way

And as I grow to love you both more and more
I realize we do not need a special invitation to come by
because there is always an open door

Mr. Ray melts my heart with his actor-like looks
because I think he is an actor right off the Andy Griffith show
His wisdom is so amazing and through words he shares it reminds me:
"We will reap what we sow."

I feel sad if I don't get to see you, hug you, and pray with you
Because what God joined between us is authentic and true

I thank God for giving me the courage months ago
To ask if I could come and visit because from this a friendship began to grow

And I will forever cherish these memories that we hold
And our stories can one day be shared and told

That God does want us to be love-related
Because with Him we know He has never been belated

He is right on time ~ allowing us to show more love
And He knew when He allowed us to develop a friendship that Mr. Ray,
Mrs. Sue, and Mary would together consist of
A good example for others to see of those who are love-related . . .

Magnify My Memory

O Lord I pray, magnify my memory in Your most mighty way
So I can speak to my sister, for I still have so much to say

As you magnify my memory, I can laugh and cry
As I rekindle all the memories that were so special for my sister and I

I can tell her, "You remember the time when we . . ."
For these memories will keep her forever so close to me

Having a sister is a true gift anyway
But having to let go too soon was the most dreadful day

So magnify my memory to help me deal with this grief and pain
For I believe this is how You can comfort me
through my magnified memory You ordain

"As a mother comforts her child so will I comfort you" Isaiah 66:13
Is the most welcoming promise You give to me whenever I feel down or blue

And then as You magnify my memory
My sister is right here again so closely

So thank You, Father above
Because as You magnify my memory I can give more and more love

For I will remember all the simple and little things in life that truly mean the most
And then the most important of all, my salvation, for which I will forever boast

Yes, it was hard to let my sister go, but I knew she, with no more suffering,
was going to be with You
And I have the ultimate promise that one day I will join You both too

So in closing, thank You, Father, again as You magnify my memory
For now I can see each and every precious memory so much more clearly . . .

I Thought of You Today . . .
In Memory of Monk

As another year passes by and it is the anniversary of your death
I know in our hearts we, too, should celebrate for it is also another anniversary
you are with God, never have to take another earthly breath

Yet, I still miss you
As I hold on and cherish simple memories that will always hold true

You had such wisdom, like when I enjoy the hummingbirds as they eat and play
I recall your reminder in my ear, "Do not feed them after September or they will
die for they need to go farther South," you would say

And as I relish in the beauty of a new rose
I find myself wanting to say, "Come look, honey" as I smell the beautiful
fragrance even from a distant as if it were placed gently up to my nose

Grieving can last for years as I have heard
And I grieve because I miss sharing my world with you, Monk,
as I now cherish each and every memorable word

The mission is still growing and changing each year
And it still and always will hold in my heart a place so dear

I even get tickled when I see all the "wish books" or magazines today
For you were so childlike as you would wish for something as you knew Melody
or Mary would make sure to send it your way

No, I haven't quit missing you and I just wanted you to know
But God still has some things in store for me to do for Him
as He reveals to me and then shows

One day we will be together again and I can see your beautiful shining face
As I hear you say, "Mama, welcome to heaven with me" and then we will share a
most perfect and loving embrace . . .

Not Just a Sitter to Me

Mrs. Donna, you are not just a sitter to me
But like another mother, but with red hair you see

I can't thank God enough for my mom finding you
Because God surely knew

The love you would always give
And our family will be grateful as long as we live

See you don't have to do all the extra things you do
But you do because you want to

And you would want your children to be treated with gentleness and grace
So for this God has a special place in heaven above
because He sees what you are truly made of

Please know we never take you for granted day in and day out
Because being just a sitter is not what it is all about

It is about God placing you in His perfect time in our way
To love me and to play with me each and every day

I love you like another mother because of the love you have shown
This special quality all your very own

So once again you are not just a sitter to me
But an angel in disguise, you see
To God we made that perfect plea

To have someone who would love our miracle child as I am a child of the King
And we knew the love, Mia Faith, too, would bring

To that special person God would select to take good care of her
And this is what we have in you, for sure

You are part of each of my first accomplishments
As each and every one are heaven sent

Mrs. Donna one day you're gonna most likely become "Nonna"
No, not just a sitter to me

But a heaven-sent gift indeed
Yes, a true angel you see
And we hope through the years we will always be
Us three:
God, you, and me . . . Mia Faith

written by my mom, Mary

Dedicated to Donna . . .
You are truly our Godsend

Paralyzed in Your Love

The dreadful day came when a gunshot entered my body
As I was trying to make a living as a taxi cab driver, you see

Then the words spoken by the doctors to me:
"You will probably be paralyzed from the waist down."
I must have been in a terrible dream
as I remember how horrible these words to me did sound

Well, a new light came on inside of me
As Jesus took my hand and held me in His loving arms so gently

Then He gave me a POWER that only comes from Him and Him alone
As He allowed me to feel paralyzed in His love
instead of words filled with anguish and excessive moans and groans

Then He gave me promise after promise in His word like:
"Now to him who is able to do immeasurably more
than all we ask or imagine according to
His power that is at work within us" Ephesians 3:20
And all it takes is to completely in Him ~ trust

From this day on I began to claim healing on my body, for I will walk again
But for now, I dwell in the presence of the Lord
so close as I am paralyzed in His love and
with Him carrying me ~ I absolutely will and can

Thank You, Father, for showing me my purpose now in life
And allowing me to walk into the hearts of the lost
as I share my miracle testimony and how You took away all my strife

May I forever be paralyzed in Your love
As I share with everyone the miracles that You still today perform and all Your
great and mighty ways You consist of . . .

Dedicated to my new brother in Christ. God is going to use his testimony in an amazing way.

The Storm Will Pass

In a moment's time it is as if your whole life has been swept away
And you could not even decide what should go or what should stay

How could everything just go so fast?
But the blessing is the memories from your home will always last

In times like these we can truly grasp the reality that it is all just stuff anyway
And it must also be a reminder to us that the only thing that will stand
is God's love today and every day

Too, there are events that happen in our lives that we can never understand
However, everything can be used to glorify God,
which is part of His ultimate plan

In tragic times like these is when you learn so much about
Neighbors, co-workers, strangers, and friends who want to help, no doubt

And again another blessing will come
For God will put new lives to befriend and He will even rekindle some

Like all storms ~ the storm will pass, my friend
And God will help you rebuild and renew your strength, courage, faith, hope,
and new dreams with a loving home He will also send . . .

So turn to God every step of this new journey you will take
For with Him as the firm foundation of any new home you lay,
moving forward, you can never make any mistake

He promises to His children,
"Never will I leave you, never will I forsake you" Hebrews 13:5
So from this day on, Father, help me use this trial in my life to glorify You
As I hold on to promise after promise in your Bible so relevant and true . . .

Dedicated to unknown friends in
Nashville and Willie and Sarah

Caleb ~ A Child's Courage

God blessed Ray and Kelly on December, 6, 2000, with Caleb, their precious son
Not knowing, like all parents, what the following days and years
would hold for this dear one

Caleb was diagnosed with a rare genetic disease
called Hurler Syndrome before the age of two
When most parents are complaining about their child being a "terrible two" and
not knowing what to do, this family had more critical decisions to make
as they asked, "Dear God, what do we do?"

At another tender age of just eighteen months old, Caleb was having a bone
marrow transplant in hopes of saving this precious boy's life
When most children are enjoying the mere innocence of being a child and their
family is not dealing with this much strife

Yet, God has used Caleb's life to teach so many around him
what true courage is all about
Giving others a new hope and a new perspective on life,
leaving little room for self-pity, no doubt

St. Jude Hospital in Memphis, Tennessee,
has been the angel God sent to Caleb and his family
For they have been there to provide an endless amount of hope and support just
like Caleb has been to others at St. Jude
dealing with their own days of uncertainty

Their faith in God has grown so much for Caleb's family daily
As they completely lean on God and place their trust in Him, solely

Caleb is now ten years young and still has many surgeries to go
But he is the most precious reminder of how much God does love us so

When you see Caleb ~ he has a beautiful porcelain doll-like face
Making it irresistible to gently place a sweet kiss, as he begins to blush,
and give him a loving embrace

*In God's Holy Word He says, "For my thoughts are not your thoughts,
neither are my ways your ways" Isaiah 55:8
For His ways are always best as He carefully molds our delicate lives
into His masterpiece of clay*

*Caleb is an angel God perfectly made to show us what true courage consists of
And, yes, his life is a delicate reminder of God's unfailing love . . .*

I go to church with this family and God gave me this special poem as a dedication to them for "keeping their faith" and seeing all the beauty Caleb's life brings to so many others

Alison ~ Dedicated Wife, Devoted Mom

*Twelve years ago, God brought Alison and Scotty to become man and wife
For together they were united as one and they began a new life*

*A few years went by and their family began
With their adorable son, Peyton, for this was God's perfect plan*

*Alison and Scotty loved being a parent to their son
And they both knew in their hearts they would never just have one*

*Then along came more precious ones ~ Ava, Chloe, and then Drew
As quickly their beautiful family in God's perfect time ~ grew*

*And when you see Alison today, she is just as beautiful as before
With her gorgeous blue eyes and a beautiful natural look
that you can never ignore*

*Having children has been her dream come true
Enjoying the simple, country life with her family to include all their farm
animals is like having their very own Lejeune zoo*

She teaches her children about caring for others
in the way she treats all the animals on their farm
And therefore; the children know about loving and giving
instead of causing someone harm

She is very creative in her own unique way
As she named the Short Stop Food Stores for Scotty
showing the important part she still plays

And Alison has always been a very good tennis player when she used to play
And who knows, she may have her very own tennis team
with her own family in the years to come one day

But for now, God is ready to bless Scotty and Alison once more
With a precious little boy due in November,
and this wonderful family is ready to pour

All their love and support to the new addition in their lives
And God must have known how special a bond this family would become
with their children of five

Yes, it is easy to see Alison as a dedicated wife, devoted mom
For no matter the circumstance, Alison is able to remain caring and calm

So as God sees you, Alison, with your love and unselfish acts of kindness
for your family
He must look down on you and say, "Alison, My child,
you are a true reflection of a dedicated wife, devoted mom
so accept My blessings as you are becoming more like Me."

Written for my friend, Scotty, for
his beautiful wife and the next poem
for his son, of whom he is so proud

Peyton ~ A Born Player

Since the day our first son, Peyton, was born into our family
We knew as we held him for the first time that he would be unique
with a gifted talent that all would see

From a very young age, he liked sports like most boys do
Yet, he loved baseball in a way like no other, for this was the beginning clue

As he grew, his love for baseball grew too
And wherever we would go he would have new fans that saw the "star quality"
that is given to very few

Last fall, he was invited to try out for a competitive baseball team in Houston
Which would now take Peyton out of his comfort zone and previous days of
casual playing would be done

Peyton can now be described as a risk taker, dedicated, motivated, determined,
and who always remains positive
For great baseball players of today can be described in the very same way
as they, too, daily strive to live

His nickname is Tiger on the team
As this family are huge LSU Tiger fans,
so this is only fitting it would seem

Peyton's team, The Banditos, went to Omaha, Nebraska, in the spring
And came home winners of the Triple Crown National Tournament
~ yes, a huge trophy they did bring

Peyton, God has blessed you with this gift of playing baseball
But never forget where you came from and with God along for the ride,
you can always stand tall

With God, He can take you places that you can never dream possible
And remember, with God, nothing is too big or too impossible

Your family is so very proud of you
But they do their best to remain humble too

So, Peyton, one day when you make your first home run in the Major League
Nod with a thanks to heaven and then take a bow
toward your entire family in the stands
for they always did believe

And never give up on the biggest dream of all
To have your name, Peyton, in the Hall of Fame
as memories of how it all started as you humbly recall . . .

Just Pray . . .

Starting a new business can come with so many unknown stresses, so what do
we do? . . . just pray
For God put His desire for us and we have to trust Him today

How about some of the unforeseen expenses that we never planned
for? . . . just pray
For God uses these obstacles to test our perseverance as our lives are constantly
on display

When tears and more tears are shed when only joy should be coming as we are
supposedly living our dream, what do we do? . . . just pray
For God has so many great things in store because you remembered to TRUST
Him yesterday and now this very day

Months pass and the business grows
And as you pause for a moment, in your heart you simply know

It was all because in the good days and in the bad days,
we took the time to . . . just pray
For this is what God's Holy Word does say

So, Father, let me stop for this moment and . . . just pray,
"Pray continued blessings upon this business as You are proving Your
sweet love with a likeness of You through prayer, they portray . . . "

My Friend Is Mia . . .

I have a new friend and her name is Mia, you see
Not just another friend, but more special because she is also a sister to me

I like her to be close so I can aggravate her some and then play with her too
Because I guess this is what most big brothers do

I know as the years go by I will become more than just a brother
I will also become a protector

Having a sister is like a dream come true
Even though at first it seemed so foreign and new

Now our family could not imagine our lives without Mia in it
For now we are a puzzle that has a perfect fit

God gave her to us in His perfect time like He does with everything
Because His best is what He will always bring

I vow to be the best big brother to Mia in the days ahead
So in my footsteps she will want to tread

I am blessed for I have Mia
My sister
My friend
Brother and Sister ~ there for each other 'til the very end

Jim ~ Businessman and Builder

To most in the small town of Hernando,
Jim is known as the businessman and builder
But to others, he is much more for he is a father, daddy daddy, a husband,
and yes, an entrepreneur

Jim knows about working hard each day
As he finds new businesses and fun things to dabble in along the way

He owns a fully loaded big, white, Chevy truck that you see him drive no more
For you only see him drive around town in his used black Toyota Tacoma,
which he probably wouldn't take a million bucks for

Jim is the kind of man who anyone could meet and like on the street
For he is as down-to-earth as anyone could ever meet

If you need any kind of work done on your home, Jim is the one to call
As he can recite a phone number in a blink of an eye, for he has memorized them all

Jim treats people fair and takes care of the ones he loves too
For he has a big heart and sees the good in people like we all should do

Jim seems to never age even though he deals with much stress
Making us all wonder ~ is he hiding some secret age remedy nonetheless

Jim can also be known as a little tight with his money
Yet behind the scenes, he will help anyone in need, but not for others to see

Yes, Jim is a businessman and builder, but also a neighbor and friend
Jim, you hold many titles, but the greatest title of all is that you are
God's child to the very end . . .

Rhonda ~ Rare Jewel

Rhonda, you are definitely a rare jewel
From your heart much love pours out like flowing fuel

You are the strong glue that keeps your family tight
And they come to you to make all their cares just right

You take very good care of Jim who is always on the go
And through so many ways, your love constantly does show

You always have a beautiful smile upon your beautiful face
With your bubbly personality, which is a testimony to others that each day you
thankfully embrace

There are not too many people in this world around
Like you, Rhonda, who is a rare jewel that Jim definitely found

Rare jewels are hard to find
And you are ONE who is a very rare kind

May God bless your life with all His magnificent rare and beautiful ways
As these blessings show you how much your Father loves you
for with each one ~ He does say,

"Rhonda, my child you are My rare jewel who I love so very much
And may you continue to shine so beautiful with each life you gently touch."

Rearview Mirror

Dedicated to Bob Black

A lady once asked, "What does God have in store for me?"
Well, a wise man once said, "Look in the rearview mirror and see."

For God has done so much in your life and mine
Helping us through trials and giving us moments to shine

He will never leave me nor forsake me . . . . Hebrews 13:5
Is a beautiful promise given in His Holy Word that so clearly

Reflects on all that God has done for you
For He only wants His best for us, which is another promise
in His Holy Word, so true

As I reflect on my life when I look in the rearview mirror
I will smile with thanksgiving, for the journey ahead
is going to be amazing, for sure

For I see Christ clearly when I look in my mirror of life from my past
And I am confident He will become clearer
as He fulfills the purpose for my life ahead at last . . .

Sweet Treat

As you begin your work week at school
May you enjoy these "sweet treats" as you refuel

Thank you for the gift of teaching this child today
And may God bless you this week in his own unique way

We are blessed because of teachers who teach with love
And these are traits that God has given you
and traits that He also consists of

You are as sweet as the treat given to you
And may you know how much you are appreciated
by these little things we do . . .

For my son, Ethan

Graduation Prayer

Dear Father above, I want to send this graduation prayer
As this graduate steps into a new chapter of their life
that You handled them with care

In today's society there is so much stress of finding a new job
Leaving many in distress and moments in sob

But Father only when You go into every interview
and hand-to-heart come along
Then only the most perfect door will open and others will be shut,
for they were all wrong

What a beautiful promise to know You only want the best for Your children
to include you and me
For You have already gone ahead and planned my course so perfectly

When we have You in our lives to bow our knees and pray
Then You will fill us with Your fulfillment of peace, love, and joy
and then send us back on our way

Therefore, we can offer this world the very best of you and me
For through this fulfillment my hope and prayer is ~ this new graduate, Christ-
confident, is ready for all the world to see . . .
And along the way, who knows, others may also come to be

A new life with Christ-confidence to portray
For we never know who is watching as our lives are on display
So thank You, Lord, for You answered this graduation prayer and used this life
to help others find their way . . .

Your Child

Dear God, I come to You to dedicate an unborn child that was never born
When today, even though I am forgiven ~ I still feel so very torn

If I am Your child ~ why do I feel so ashamed?
When I should remember You died on a cross and this past sin has been forgiven
so somehow help me this promise to proclaim

As I am reminded that I will meet Your Child one day in heaven, you see
As I dedicate my time on earth living completely for Thee

We can use all bad for Your good if we will just allow
Barriers to come down and Your glory to come flowing in so perfectly timed ~
just now

Help me help other women or young girls who need to hear from someone who
has walked in their shoes
And how Christ will help them make the right decision that will take away any
doubt or long-lasting unwanted blues

And in Your perfect time, You will once again send me Your Child,
for you know the desire of my heart
And this child will know the importance of a life from the very start

As I dedicate this child back to You in thanksgiving
Dear God, here is Your child so "perfectly and wonderfully made" as
Your child resembles You and Your child is a reminder of your beautiful promise
to me of forgiving . . .

Dedicated to a new friend
God placed in my life
for whom to write this poem

The Joy of Joni

Since this is your first Mother's Day
I just could not miss the opportunity to say

That you are the best mommy in all the earth
And I sure hope I am completely worth

Every sleepless night I still go through
For one day this will pass, but I will always still need you

For no one can love me better than Daddy or especially you, my mommy
And when others look at me I am so proud it is a reflection of you they see

They say the best things are worth the wait
And Jesus sure did show up on time for He is never late

I make all your worries go away when you see how happy I can be
For Jesus made me this way like laughing out loud so happy and bubbly

And I know your favorite month of the year is July
For I came into this world like a gentle precious lullaby

Don't worry, Mommy, when I go to daycare
For the long hours you give goes along with me so I never go bare

I love all the stories you read to me
And, who knows, maybe one day you can share our favorite story
The Joy of Joni

For Gene and Susan—first Mother's Day

ENCOURAGING AND INSPIRATIONAL POEMS

There are so many variations of titles that God has given me and so many different topics throughout these months to write about. Some deal with personal experiences and many are things I have never dealt with in my own life, but somehow God inspired me to write. These different topics may help someone dealing with this in their personal life. You may have a friend or family member who has some of these same struggles and enjoyments that you could share this book with too. I have so many favorites in this section, but a few that immediately come to mind are: "Another Chance," "Counterfeit," "Humbleness," "Miscarriage," "Our Five Senses," "Secret Ingredient," "Sacrifice of a Soldier," "Song of an Ocean Wave," "The Cookies," "The First Step," "The Porch," "Trust," "The Sweet South," "We Didn't Even Ask," What If," and "Your Time." My prayer is that you find some of your favorites that you can share with those you love, and allow the *Potter's Hand* to speak to them in a very special and loving way.

A Heart Transplant

So many young and old lives need a heart transplant to help them live a better
life in their days ahead
For one day we will stand before the Lord
as your Holy Word has promised and said

We will either die and live an eternal life of damnation and hell
Or because of our heart transplant, live an eternal life in heaven with all the
majesty that, Almighty God, Your Holy Word does tell

With our heart transplant we will look at everyday things in a new way
With more compassion, empathy, love, gentleness,
with the certainty of our new lives molded by
You, the potter, into a beautiful form of clay

We will feel alive and new
For our heart transplant will give us a new view

Of how our purpose in this blink-of-an-eye time on earth
Can become so beautiful and wonderful for, You, our Heart Surgeon as being
Your child is definitely worth

Every storm or hardship we face
For one day we will finally meet You face to face and feel Your ultimate embrace

So, thank You, Father, for this new heart You gave to me
As I yearn to become a reflection of You in all Your Beauty and Majesty . . .

A Simple Kiss . . .

You will never know what a simple kiss means from you
As we get hectic with our lives and our children, it is still nice to show love
even in these simple things we do

A simple kiss can say, "I love you," "I believe in you,"
and "I am always here to support,"
For there are so many responsibilities and a simple kiss can keep me strong when
some days I feel I may fall a little short

A simple kiss holds so much power whether at the beginning or end of the day
And I thank You, God, for each simple kiss that is given to me
for in my heart it is like getting the most beautiful arranged bouquet . . .

Anniversary Prayer

My anniversary prayer today
Is that God take care of you in His very special way

My life has been blessed because I have had your love with me
through all these years
And we shared days full of laughter and some days full of tears

No matter how old I become ~ I want you by my side
As God shows me new and exciting ways to show love, because my love for you
will always deep within my heart abide . . .

Adoption

Grief may consume a woman's heart as she longs to have a baby
A dream of one day becoming a mother she can clearly see

Events happen that seem to crush this dream like turning off a light
However you may not see it now, but God will give you new sight

This grief may never go away, but God will give you new hope
Like looking for the first time at the stars through a telescope

Things are not always as they seem
For in God's perfect time and in His time alone He will deem

A new dream of becoming a mother or even a father He will give
As there are so many precious children young and old that live

Without the love a family can offer
A place to call home that they can always be sure

God must have created adoption for a way we can finally express our love
Just like He adopted us into His family so we can be a part of

Him . . . and then you can begin to live
in a way that is a reflection of Him, you see
Just like an adopted child will be a reflection of your love clearly

The love you overwhelming show
And from now on this child will always know

This is a true mom and dad
And it is all because God so lovingly had
A plan in store when He created this adoption
As He looked upon this new reunion created in His own image
and said, "Well done."

Another Chance

Times in our lives when we really mess up
And we feel so dry is our cup . . .

Oh, how I wish my cup overfloweth
Well, God all knowing, knoweth

God, will You give me one more chance?
For You know all about my circumstance

God lovingly does
Only through His ultimate love and forgiveness and not just because

"My child, never think your life could be so bad
For, I, Christ died for all your sins you will and have had."

Times go by and seasons change and again we make mistake after mistake
Because of poor decisions that we make

Surely, God will not give me this second chance
But only He will because He knows all about my circumstance

He doesn't keep a tally sheet and say, "Sorry, your cup will have to stay dry,"
Instead He forgives us and holds us close in His arms without questioning why

So when you and I make these sinful decisions in our lives
That ultimately only brings so much strife

Don't ask, "God, will You give me one more chance?"
Or, "God will You give me a second chance?"

Instead allow God to say, "Come to me, my child,
for I alone will give you another chance."

As you Wake . . .

Welcome, My child, to a new day . . .
As you wake ~ remember throughout your day, I am never far away

No matter what bad or good comes to you
Hold on to My promise through the pages of My Holy Word ~
each one so true!

And when you close your eyes tonight
Know that I am watching and praying over you ~ for you are
"fearfully and wonderfully made" in my sight . . .
Psalm 139:14

Birthday Blessing

No matter whether young, middle aged, or old
Your birthday is a time to celebrate the gift of your life as you hold

A birthday blessing in your hands and heart
Of a love from Jesus who wants to always be a part

Of your joyous celebrations like your birthday and even your sorrows too
Because He already knows what did and is going to happen to me and you

He can give you good things in your life you never dreamed possible
For He wants to give us His great blessings
because for Him nothing is impossible

And when the sorrows of life come our way
He will comfort with peace, love, and gentleness never felt before, as He is truly
never far away

He will bless us as we develop an intimate relationship with Him as we grow
For we long to be closer to Him and with wisdom He gives,
we can with confidence know

The purpose for our lives He has for me and you
Which will bring more days of joy, for we now have a clearer view

And when the next birthday comes around the following year
It will never be just another birthday with a simple birthday cheer

It will be a reminder that a birthday blessing has been given to me
For Christ loves me and wants me to live my life for Him,
for there is never any guarantee

So, thank You Lord, today, for this birthday blessing
And may my life be a true blessing to others as my love for You I
am daily expressing . . .

Bow the Knee

When it gets to a point when you do not know which way to go
Well go down, my friend, so the Father can show

Humble yourself in a way you may never have known and bow the knee
For on our knees is where we can finally see

See a love that is felt so deep
For with Christ we finally meet

And give it all to Him while I bow the knee
And allow Him to replace all my grief with a comfort so complete and so real
between Him and me

And sometimes God needs to bring us to our knees
For us to realize this world is not about you or me

We do have a purpose on this earth and it is to help others come to know Him
A new life filled with joy, hope, and love instead of a life so grim

And even in the best days of our lives, my friend, let us be
The ones who do not forget to bow the knee

Because with praises the hard times do not seem so bad
And we begin to have more days with hope and laughter and less so sad

In these days of a troubled world of so much sin
Let us all bow the knee and let our Father in . . .

For in this reverence of how much we do not deserve His love
We will begin to realize the love and forgiveness He completely consists of

So spend time with Him as you bow the knee
And see how your life is transformed to be

More Christ-like walking daily hand in hand with a Father and a Friend
Because I bowed the knee
I now can boldly forever stand!

CAN in Cancer

The word CAN is in the dreadful word cancer for a reason
Just like trials in our lives will only last for a season

Cancer can not steal special friendships
It CAN teach us to treasure them more and more and never let them slip

Cancer can not weaken love
It CAN strengthen us to love with the kind of love that only Christ consists of

Cancer cannot corrode our faith or shatter our hope
It CAN develop our faith with a perseverance as we learn to cope

Cancer cannot take away precious memories
It CAN help us cherish each memory as they are now viewed differently

Cancer cannot quench the spirit of God who lives within us
It CAN grow this personal relationship on a deeper level as we learn how to
simply trust

Cancer can not reduce eternal life
It CAN give us the promise of eternal life in heaven when we accept Christ with
no suffering or strife

There are so many wonderful CAN's in cancer
And we can always turn to Christ who holds the most perfect answer

Allow this trial to bring out all the CAN's in you
And hold onto promise after promise in God's word as we practice a living of
CAN, Father, only for You, so peaceful, loving, faithful, and true . . .

Cautious with Criticism

Today it is very rare to find
Words truly spoken that are loving and kind

We can be so quick to criticize the other one
Instead of stepping back and realizing the hurt that we have done

We are to encourage one another
and build each other up . . . 1Thessalonians 5:11
Therefore, changing our criticism into confidence in them and their abilities with
encouraging words that only fill their cup

Do not let worry enter into your sinful world today
For worry only causes your faith to falter as if to say,

"God, there is no way You can handle this situation or storm that has arose,"
So I will worry and then worry some more and even choose to stick my nose

Into this storm or situation that is none of my concern
And add a little criticism instead of using this as a lesson of faith to learn

For a person may turn to you for loving advice
But the moment you add criticism instead of compliments,
the next time they will think twice

See, they may be having a difficult time enough as it is in their life
And their wish was to gain some confidence from this loved one
instead of even more strife

So if you are ever tempted to criticize
Be cautious, for God in His time will knock you down to size

You can never sprinkle enough love and encouragement
into another life like Jesus did
But oh, how wonderful to be compared to Jesus
with the criticism you, now, choose to rid

Yes, be cautious with criticism the next time you are given the chance
For God will test you to see if your faith can withstand this temptation of
criticism in another's circumstance

Allow your words softly spoken to be healing to the bones Proverbs 16: 24
With beautiful melodies and the most confident and complimentary tones

For Christ has given you the power
So from now on, choose not to be cautious
But confident in Christ as He reigns from His almighty and constant tower . . .

Chasing after the Wind

Ecclesiastes 2:17–26

During a work week we have the same old routine
And we sometimes wonder what does all the constant work for my life mean?

All we seem to do is work and then work some more
Putting work before family and others just doing one more worthless chore

All we are doing is just chasing after the wind
Instead of placing our faith in God and allowing His work to fully in us descend

Into our lives and begin to make a difference in this world of routine and
confusion and unhappiness we all feel
For we are chasing after the wind and this feeling of hopelessness is so real

We end up working ourselves to death and leaving it all for someone else anyway
Instead of working for Christ and allowing Him to work in us
as He directs each day

We become so stressed that even when we lay our heads down at night
Our minds cannot rest, which is meaningless in God's sight Ecclesiastes 2:22–23

Satan uses work full of overtime hours to wear us down
So we never have time to show up for church, to find out about doing God's
work here and abound

Our communities and our world need us full of God's purpose
to help them find their way
As more and more people go through each day with no purpose or hope,
which leads them to go astray

God has a purpose for each of our lives and it begins with knowing Him
on a personal level, my friend
And then you will leave chasing after the wind behind
and start living for Christ as your new life with Him will ascend . . .

Coffee or Christ

Most days as soon as we step out of bed we think, "It is time to make the coffee."
Seldom do we begin with thanksgiving for another day
Christ has allowed us to see

We become addicted to the caffeine that wakes us up
Instead of beginning our day by allowing Christ to fill our cup

Today, Lord, help me choose You completely instead
As soon as I carefully arise from my warm comfortable bed

Teach me to fast as I seek Your face to give me everything I need
As I take time on Your Holy Word, today, to feed

Coffee or Christ ~ which will it be?
I will gladly choose Christ,
as I am reminded of all He has done for undeserving me . . .

Confirmed Reservation

Do you have a confirmed reservation today?
When you accept Christ as your personal Savior,
then you indeed should never dismay

For this is the only confirmed reservation you will ever need
And from now on, fear should never reside within thee

The most dangerous thing to our faith is fear
In these times, we need to remember that God is always near

And no matter what we face this side of earth today or in the future
We can survive absolutely anything with a strong faith of one thing we can
always be sure

Jesus will never leave or forsake us
And all He wants for us to do in all our being is love and trust

Completely in Him for "I go and prepare a place for you;
I will come back and take you to be with me" is a promise for His children so true

"In my Father's house are many rooms"
Where infinite love dwells and every good thing blooms

Jesus also said, "I am the way the truth and the life.
No one comes to the Father except through Me."
What an amazing reservation where we can dress so elegantly
when at last we accompany Thee

An elegance of a life filled with winning souls t
o share eternity in this mansion too
For we should want this for everyone when we live an unselfish life
where we lavishly live for you

Therefore anytime you encounter the hardest decision you have ever faced
Remember being in God's presence with the Holy Spirit is the most perfect place

Oh how humbling to think Christ is precisely preparing a mansion for you and me
For we are so unworthy, yet God loves us beyond any measure or degree

Be confirmed of your own reservation before it is too late
For without your confirmed reservation you will not be allowed to savor the
most perfect plate

We can never earn our way into heaven
For it is a free gift to everyone who when Christ calls
~ we gladly and humbly accept His invitation

What an abundant life we can live as we are confirmed to join
Our Eternal Father in heaven for the #1 reservation
that we do not want to miss or avoid

So now we have work to do, my friend, that includes you and me
For we want to come to our confirmed reservation with much to offer our
Father, not empty handed or half heartedly

For only the best deserve the honor of a confirmed reservation
However, heaven would be quite empty if this were the case; therefore, it is not
due to all we have or have not done

It is only confessing the sinner that you are and accept Christ to live in your
heart and save you from your sin
Recognizing He paid the ultimate price when He died on that cross and now I
have a new life where the Holy Spirit resides within

Still we face challenge after challenge as Satan lurks
in hopes that we will turn away
However, you already have a confirmed reservation in His lamb's book of life,
where we eagerly await for Him to say

"Come, my dear child, for you have a confirmed reservation
to spend eternity with me;
Therefore, enter in for I want to show you the mansion
that has been prepared specifically for thee . . ."

Scripture reference: John 14:1–6

Consumed

Things and more things of this world daily consume you and me
Figuring out in our shallow minds how to get more constantly

How to afford this house, purchase a new car for a teenager,
or paying the next bill
Never taking the time to rest in the Lord and just Be Still Psalm 46:10

Our focus today should get a humbling makeover
Rare to find like in a blanket of grass a four-leaf clover

Become consumed with knowing God on a more intimate level
Instead of this world of more things that come from the devil

Truly wanting to be in His presence if only for a short time in a day
Will allow you to see perspectives in a brand-new way

Coming to Him in grief is sometimes how He must get our attention
For in these hard times finally God is mentioned

After the hard times pass, continue to spend time
just praising Him for all He has done for you
And claim promise after promise in scripture that still today holds so true

Become consumed in souls to win
To save the lost of this world from all the deadly sins

Consumed in loving Him in ways you never have before
And He will begin to reveal himself more and more

Finally desires of your heart will come true
For see, you allowed God to put those desires there just for you

Becoming consumed with God and all His love
Is like placing your hand out and embracing a beautiful white dove

In awe and more awe is how you feel mostly
For now I can accomplish anything as Christ is right beside me

Consumed, consumed, and more consumed with you, my Father above
For in you and you alone, I feel your consistent and unfailing love . . .

Contagious

Avoid, avoid, avoid anyone who is sick and could be contagious
Due to our busy lifestyles, becoming sick only produces a big mess

We become a burden and possibly have to depend on someone else
for a little help during times when we are sick
Yet, maybe God needs to use this time to settle us down and refocus,
for the reality is this is a test and not a trick

So when it comes to illness, contagious is a deadly word indeed
Filled with only bad thoughts on which we can feed

If we flip the coin for a moment and compare contagious on the other side
It can be a wonderful gift to be "Contagious for Christ"
for it will only be an extraordinary ride

Others will cling to you for they cannot get enough of the love you give
As they watch your life as you daily live

You will hear them say with their mouths and minds
"I want exactly what this person has and to become 'Contagious for Christ'
so God, please, help me find."

This peace and joy that is so hard to describe
Making you feel like you can climb any mountain for you feel so alive

And no matter what storm comes your way
You realize the Potter is carefully forming His clay

And you do not resist like you did before
For molding you into what He wants you to become will give you so much more

So the next time you hear the word contagious ~ perk up in a new way
And ask God to allow you to become
"Contagious for Christ"
as He forms you into His masterpiece of clay . . .

Counterfeit

When you hold in your hands a counterfeit 100 dollar bill
At first glance and even for a while it seems to you that it is real

However, if you begin to analyze it a little more
Then you can understand what it is really for

When you feel the texture and hold it up to the light
Is when you finally realize that it is a fake and it is not all right

You feel deceived and taken for a fool
For someone created this counterfeit bill
because they do not want to follow any rule

Well, step back for a moment and see
all the Counterfeit Christians walking around
They are sitting next to you at church and all abound

For on the outside they seem authentic and true
However, in the blink of eye they will turn and get the best of you

When their lives are finally held up to a light
Is when they resist with all their might
And sometimes even put up a fight

For see it is a hypocrite in disguise
Moving along the way and ruining so many lives

It has to make God so very sad
For there is nothing counterfeit about Him and His love is not just a fad

It is happening every moment of every day
And all He wants us to do is humbly accept Him and follow Him today

If you have lived a deceptive counterfeit life ~ it is never too late
For once in your life, truly accept Christ as your personal Savior and get your life
straight

He will never abandon you if you mess up now and then and then mess up again
For He paid the ultimate sacrifice when He suffered on that cross
to save us from all sin

So release your counterfeit life
For you will be caught one day and it will cut as sharp as a knife

Counterfeit is exactly what Satan loves
Because deception is one of the traits he is quite proud of

Turn Counterfeit into Character
For an abundant life from now on you can be sure

One day somehow our true person will appear
So will you shine like a rare diamond or hide in fear?
It is never too late, so allow God, to turn this into . . . your Character year

Scripture reference: Luke 12:2

Country at Heart

No matter where I go or who I meet ~ I will always be country at heart
For this is where my roots are and where my life did so preciously start

Being country at heart means so many wonderful things
Like caring, hospitality, down-to-earth, simple,
and all the enjoying qualities life can bring

I thank God for making me country at heart
With a warm smile and a sincere "ya'll are welcome anytime" and so many other
sweet expressions that will always be like a most beautiful work of art . . .

Deacon's Prayer

God has selected not just the twelve, but you
To serve as a deacon, which is a beautiful gift of serving given to only few

May He guide you in your deacon role
As you lead with humbleness, gentleness, and love as you make being like
Jesus your ultimate goal

God, bless this servant that You have chosen
through the words of this deacon prayer
And may he become more like You each day as his love for You, boldly,
with thankfulness, through actions and not just words, he does declare . . .

This poem is dedicated to my friend, Bro. Bob and his wife Gloria, as he became a new deacon at our church. He is a beautiful example of God's love.

Developing Faith

In James 1:2 it talks about considering it pure joy when your faith is tested
For in God and God alone our whole life is vested

Then back in Romans 5:3, it describes to rejoice in our sufferings
For in them they develop perseverance, perseverance ~ character
and character ~ hope
all ultimately for us closer to Christ they bring

My friend, you nor I will never just fall into faith one day
It will come with a high price, but the gift received,
will be priceless as your life will display

Trusting God no matter what
Is much easier said than done as we long to use what He just taught

And God reminds us in His word in which we feed
That He can do some magnificent things in and with our lives
if we can have the faith of a tiny little mustard seed

If you ever have the desire to move to the next level of your faith
as your grow in your walk which seems to be very few
Be ready for the ride of your life, yes, with a trial as a major part of this
developing faith you will do

When you develop an attitude of,
"I want to serve You, Lord, and love You even more,"
Then no matter what comes your way,
you have made the decision in Christ alone to adore

Then my friend, He will begin to use your life in a mighty way
Because in Him you have found the hope and now your developed faith
will begin to play

A bigger role for when you tell the mountain to move
You can be assured now with Christ and Christ alone,
to man there is nothing you need to prove

Ultimately, when you can one day fall so in love with the Lord
that no matter what might come
Is when all the rest will fall into place and He will use your life in all your days
and not just a few or some

Developing faith is a privilege in disguise
For in faith from any trial we can now arise

And see all that we can use to glorify You
For You are so worthy and I can't wait to see
what my developed faith in the future with reverence and humbleness do . . .

Scripture Reference: Luke 10:27

Did I Tell You I Love You ? . . .

Did I tell you I love you, today, by my desire to work
as I make a living for our family?
Though I may not be great with the exact words
"I love you," my service is the way I say it mostly

Did I tell you I love you by the prayer I gave God to bless your day?
For I love you more than mere words could briefly say

So may I tell you that I love you through this poem given from me to you
And may we share pages from our storybook
as together new chapters unfold with more and more new ways
to say I love you, too

Dream

Dream a dream today
For in this dream some just may

Prosper from a dream you never let go
For in this dream came an amazing perseverance you did bestow

Dreams can keep us so alive
For lies ahead of us within grasp something on which we strive

Challenges will definitely come our way
However this will help us never take it for granted one day

For it can become as big as you want if you just believe
Through hard work and never letting go we can soon achieve

The dreams that will last a lifetime are the ones that come from above
For God will plant these dreams in our lives as a way to show His love

See, these dreams always seem impossible to man
Which is why God made these so big, because only with Him we can

Achieve the most impossible dream that some will ever know
For God was so evident in this impossible dream and through this many new
seeds you did sow

So allow God to turn you into a dreamer today
For through this dream He can use your life in a mighty way

Remember nothing is impossible for the One who created you and me
For He lives within us and can supernaturally be

The dream maker who through our lives will use
To bring the glorious and beautiful news

Of a Christ who wants the biggest dream of ever to come true
And that is to spend eternity with His creation and that means . . . me and you!

Everlasting Aroma

May I have Your everlasting and beautiful aroma everywhere I go
And may my life be an image of You as each seed I plant and sow

I want to be the fragrance of life as I share the good news of You
And give me the courage to shine so beautiful for You, Christ,
through and through

For I love Your everlasting aroma that I smell each day
And I long to share this aroma with others as You help them find their way . . .

2 Corinthians 2:14–15

Every Day Is a Gift

How precious life is as every day is a gift . . .
One where we can truly lift

Others up with a hug, a smile, or a kiss
Or a romantic gesture that can be, oh so bliss . . .

Why go through each day as if it is so mundane
And feel most days due to stress that we could literally go insane?

Don't waste another day in this way
Instead open life like a delicate present where we may

Live like there is no tomorrow
Just joy and laughter without sorrow

We have a purpose as we are given this next day
One where we can absolutely play

Such an important role in bringing one more soul to Christ
through the witness we give
And treating it as a gift in the way we truly live

So as you close your day given in prayer
Remember to thank God for this gift of another day
that you hopefully handled with care . . .

Eyes and Feet

(Lesson on Contentment and Thanksgiving)

Moments happen in our lives that impact us for years to come
Whether it be a big event or a simple phrase
given through words of wisdom to some

God used my brother-in-law, Dennis, to teach me a lesson
on contentment and thanksgiving
For in my immature years, I went on and on about how much happiness a
different color of eyes to me would bring

God blessed me with beautiful brown eyes just like He wanted for me
And I am so blessed because He also gave me the ability with these same
beautiful brown eyes to see

I complained as I wished I had been given the gorgeous green eyes
that my father had
And as my brother-in-law quietly listened, he became intently sad

His reply changed my heart in an instant, you see
As he began sharing this beautiful story of wisdom to me

He replied, "Once there was a man
who saw these very expensive shoes in a store window,
And he went on and on how he just had to have these shoes
so to all he could show

How prosperous and important a man he was as he walked along the street
He felt this deep desire to have these shoes until God got his attention as he
looked upon the man with no feet."

Dennis said no more and he needed to say no more to me
For this was a life lesson of contentment and thanksgiving that I clearly did see

May we be content with all the blessings we are given
And use the words of wisdom to help others understand contentment and
thanksgiving making our lives daily worth living . . .

Father, Friend, Master, and now Manager

I have always considered You my Father over all
As your word tells me how on You, I can always call

As my relationship developed more intimately,
I then began to call You my very best friend
As You always have Your love and an ear, in Spirit, to lend

For so many years, I had a career of my own
with managers that would come and go
Some really great to work for and then others it may have been nice not to know

I never in my wildest dreams would ever think
I would be working full time for the King
As each day Your presence near me, I love to fully cling

Now my life feels full of purpose to change lives
As You guide me through each door, I am determined to make a difference
in this world as I strive

Strive each day that I wake
Not forgetting to thank You for all my blessings and then carefully make

All the right decisions with the book of Mama's life, the poetry,
the M.O.M. Ministry, and the Guatemala mission
For when these have changed lives for Your glory and my work on earth is done

Then I will finally meet my Father, Friend, Master, and now Manager
face to face
And I know I will never want to let go of Your loving and infinite embrace

So Father and Manager help me to work full time with gladness for You
So others will come to know You as their personal Savior too

Yes, it is all for You . . .

From This Day Forward . . .

From this day forward our new life will begin together
And I could never have dreamed or imagined anything better

You finish my thoughts with your words
As if each thought I have you somehow previously heard

You know what my facial expressions mean
For you alone have carefully studied each one you have seen

God gave us something special in our true love
And He hand selected you for me and you are far greater
than I could have ever dreamed of

Hopefully, we can share these beautiful memories for many years
With our children whether one, two, or four that God gives us to rear

And today I want to strive from this day forward on
To dedicate a new part of me to you as we will cherish memories
like our most favorite song

As I love God more each day
I can, from this day forward, find more perfect ways to say

I love you . . . yes, From This Day Forward . . .
I will always love you . . .

Gentle Breeze

As you sit in a rocker on a front porch
In the heat of summer at times your skin can feel a bit torched

However in the most perfect time you can be comforted by a gentle breeze
As if God is there to fan you and bring some perfect-timed ease

As workers put a hard day of labor in the heat
They can find comfort under a shade tree with a gentle breeze
as they take a much-needed break on a shaded seat

When you spend endless hours lying on the sand at the beach
With no shade around, it is an ongoing gentle breeze that is always within reach

God surrounds us through His touch of a gentle breeze like a perfect embrace
Therefore; we can feel His reminder through anything we may have to face

A gentle breeze can almost be like a gentle whisper that God gives
Reminding us, once again, of His love as long as we shall live

Thank You, God, for each gentle breeze that You have given in every season of
my life and in each day ahead
As I am reminded in your Holy Word about what you have said,

"I will never leave you nor forsake you" Hebrews 13:5
And God can use a gentle breeze as a perfect reminder
of a promise that still holds true . . .

Furry Friends

God blesses us with furry friends like a dog or a cat
Who live the good life, playing and eating, and sometimes becoming lazy
as they get rather fat

They bring laughter when sadness enters our heart
And without even realizing it through their unselfish love and without a word
they become such a vital part

A vital part of our lives as we depend on them and they depend on us
And they only bring more joy and in them we can always trust

They love to be praised and shown a little more love
Making them just like us as these are similar qualities we consist of

Yes, our furry friends can teach us so much in our busy days
And they are always there to offer more love and yes, time to play

Thank You, God, for my furry friend You gave to me
And help me to embrace another way You show love
as through my furry friend . . .
I now see

Glasses to See

Dear Lord, please give me glasses to see
All Your wondrous things ahead that display all Your majesty

At times in my life, things just seem so unclear
So I need Your glasses to see so I will not have to move forth in fear

Other times I get so busy with all the things happening in a day
That my glasses have become foggy and dirty,
so help me take them off, clean them, and place them back on
so I can again find my way

With Your glasses to see the map will seem clearer to understand
And we will not waste as much time, but instead head on a straight path
to the Promised Land

There is so much confusion and turmoil in our world today
And if I wore Your glasses to see, I could discover all You want me to do and say

They could even be the transition kind
So no matter rain or sunshine, with Your glasses to see,
I would still be able to find

All the beauty around me that You still show that I once took for granted
But with Your glasses to see, it is all here for me to enjoy ~ all of it so enchanted!

And Your glasses will never need adjusting and they will never fall from my face
For closer is Your perfection for us to finally embrace

When I go to read from Your Holy Word
Your glasses to see will give new meaning
and when You speak it will now be heard

From the moment I step out of bed
It will be your small, still voice that has said,

"You, My child, will need My glasses to see
For today, you have chosen to allow your life to fully be

A reflection of your Father above and with My glasses to see
The purpose for your life, today, will magnify for you, child, more clearly . . ."

Golden Apples

You know the saying ~ an apple a day will keep the doctor away
There may be some truth, as the apple can represent encouraging words we say
Like "golden apples on a silver tray" Proverbs 25:11

This is how our words spoken to one another can become
Each time we open our mouth to speak every word and not just some

Just imagine apples of gold in settings of silver
Where love only dwells through our words;
therefore, no room for anger to stir

This is how God wants us to
"encourage one another and build each other up" 1 Thessalonians 5:11
So He can over pour His blessings into our dry cup

A golden apple will never decay
And we will become so RICH in Christ as through our lives He will display

For see, our words of encouragement and of love
is exactly what Jesus has already shown
And they can be so "sweet to the soul and healing to our bones"
Proverbs 16:24

Allow our words to become that of golden apples
As Christ speaks through us as His living examples . . .

Happy Birthday

Nothing is more special than your birthday
An extremely delightful day when so many others will say

How important your life has surely been
A day to allow so much love and sunshine in . . .

And no matter your age whether young or old
We all have a childlike quality with our own unique life to be told

And deep down nothing makes us feel more special
than for others to remember our special day
Like getting a beautiful array of flowers
~ how pleasant and unexpected this bouquet!

So the next time you get the chance
Do not think of a birthday as a mere glance

Like "Oh, it is just another day."
But instead, "Thank you, Father, for this birthday
and help my life from now on to display."

A reflection that I care about others with more gratitude and love
Because these are the qualities that You consist of . . .

Thank You for forming me in my mother's womb so long ago
And giving me this "Happy Birthday" as Your way to show
Your love for me and from this birthday on I want others to know

It is the best "Happy Birthday" ever
Because in the days ahead it will be Jesus and me forever . . .

Hold Your Hand

My child, place your hand in My hand
As together, I have breathtaking places to take you all across this land

There is much work to be done
as you become a "co-laborer with me" 1 Corinthians 3:9
And I must hold your hand so you can fully see
and there will be less temptation to flee

See child, if I allowed you to only hold My hand as we go along
Then many times when you feel uncomfortable or unsure,
you would want to let go, but as I hold your hand,
I will never steer you wrong

I never said fulfilling your purpose I have for you
Would be easy or even quick enough; that is why the hands I hold are very few

Remember, I already know the plans I have for you and it is not to harm you,
but prosper you Jeremiah 29:11
So, please, relax as I gently hold your hand each step of the way through

And the ultimate prize will be won, you see
For along the way, I will make it fit like a beautiful puzzle so perfectly

Yes, I must hold your hand
So the roads will not be bumpy or treacherous, as I will make your paths straight
and this will be pleasing to Me, but not always man

And if you ever want to pull away because you are afraid
Remember, My child, to stop and pray and I will remind you of the ultimate
sacrifice of love that was paid

And I will never leave you, nor forsake you,
and My promise is you will feel Hebrews 13:5
Complete joy, peace, and My amazing love that with you will always be real
And you will come to realize your life is moving toward your purpose
on earth to fulfill . . .

May I hold your hand?

How Can I Ever Thank You?

My God, how can I ever thank You?
For recent talents and blessings that at one time seemed so foreign and new

I want my life on this earth to count for something more than just a paycheck
I want to leave a legacy of love and for serving You,
a life that will always reflect

Reflect my gratitude and praise for You, my Heavenly Father,
for all the mercy and grace You show toward me
And I want each day to count for You and each one where I more clearly see

Just how You are molding me into a child You can be proud of
One filled with excitement of pleasing a Father with His infinite love

And as I reflect in years to come
No matter how challenging the journey may seem to some

I want to make a difference in the lives You allow me to touch
Where they can see that I love You, my Father, so very much

So for each new gift and talent You trust me to use for Your glory
Through each one I hope to profess my heartfelt gratitude as I share our story

For I realize I can never thank You enough as long as I live
But I can surely try my best through all You allow me to give

So how then can I ever thank You
Is an expression that is completely impossible to do

But I know when we take the time to try
Is when You give so much more of You, for now we ask less and less, "Why?"

The journeys in life can be turbulent and tried
But You need for us to endure in our strength like when You suffered and died

So Father I want to humbly thank You right now
For You will use my life one day somehow

For Your glory and Your glory alone
As people may have never known

God, how can I ever thank You
For sparing my life and for the promise of spending eternity with you too?

No, I can never thank You, but I thank You still
For each day my life is a journey I want because You are there with me
~ Your presence so real

So, I thank You . . . I thank You
And until the day I take my last breath I will say, "How can I ever thank You?"

Humbleness

Humbleness~ how do I even begin?
See, it is quality that God will honor 'til the end

He despises pride and arrogance
And He will rid us of this stance

See, when we become a child of the King
Which seems today to be quite a rare thing
God will one day bring

Chapters in our lives that we just can't understand why
And we constantly try

To figure it all out because surely I can fix this on my own
When all God wants us to do is realize this is something He has known

Then finally He has to bring us to our knees
And have us cry out, "Lord, please help me!"

Then this is where He will begin
To mold us into what He wants us to become
Because we opened the door and finally let Him in
And He will remind us that He gave His one and only son

He wants to use us in quite a mighty way
To help others come to know Him one day
And give Him all the glory today and every day

See, being humble is honoring God not just every now and then
But every moment of a day as we constantly sin

Be careful as pride will try to creep back in
As Satan tries to trick us into thinking all our successes come from within

It is so easy to receive a compliment
As we can all use the sweet sentiment

But just always be on guard in your heart
As we look to heaven above and say,
"Thank You, God, for being the most important part."

Being humble is a quality obtained
Through trials and tribulations we have sustained
As long as we maintain
Becoming more and more in love with our Savior
And allow Him to find favor

He will take us places that we have never even known
As we rekindle the ultimate sacrifice that He has shown

Remember ~ stay faithful and true
As I close this poem given from Him to me to you
You can see I have had my own testimonies to go through

Places in my life
That cut as sharp as a knife

And now God always gets the glory
As I share always our story

So as you, too, become humble
Do not be afraid to stumble

Because it has been said, "When you stumble, make it part of the dance"
Because God does give us this second chance . . .

I Honor You . . .

In the middle of May on a Friday afternoon,
an almost twenty-year career came to an end
Yet when it was all said and done, I turned to You in praise, my Trusted Friend

For I have been saying for some time now
For You, in Your perfect time, to finally allow

The opportunity to work for You full time in several different ministries
Knowing good will that this huge salary would go away
and in ministry it is for a much smaller fee

But the rewards it offers knowing that so many people need You
Is like precious rubies, silver, and gold with complete joy and happiness, too

For our rewards will come in heaven
As we reach one, hundreds, thousands, or maybe seven

And it is not about the money anyway
It is helping people come to Christ so they can live the most abundant life today
With a promise of eternity in heaven for them some day

Yes, the getting there may have some treacherous roads ahead
But, I have You as my guide and I know exactly what You have said,

You will never leave me nor will You ever forsake me . . . Hebrews 13:5
And this is a testimony You will allow others to see

I am still amazed at how peaceful I feel
Which reminds me that it has come from You and it proves that You are so real

The old me would have broken down and asked, "How will we ever make it?"
Yet the new me gives little thought and is so anxious with all I want to do for
You that I rarely have time to sit

It is like a child at Christmastime who has so many toys
"Which one do I open first?" for there are so many ministries
that bring me such joy

All I can really say at this point in awe is, "I honor You"
And I want to fly like a mighty eagle with a mission of completely serving too

For You have been so good to unworthy me
As You knew all along that one day I would want to serve Thee

So, "I Honor You
I Honor You
My Father, my very Best Friend, I Honor You . . ."

I Took the Gift

You may wonder exactly what gift did I take . . .
Well, it is the only gift that will absolutely make

A difference in the way you daily live
And an extra expression of love that you freely give

This gift of salvation is completely free
If we believe Jesus died on that cross to save you and me

And all we have to do is ask for forgiveness and receive
This gift that He wants everyone to have when you can honestly say, "I believe."

How could someone love us so much for all the wrong we have done?
Yet, God allowed Jesus to brutally die on a cross, yes, His one and only Son

My mind cannot fathom a love He must have for us that is so deep
A love that He wants us to share with others and not just keep

So if you are tired of trying to figure life out on your own
Then receive Christ as your Savior so you can feel this incredible love
that He has shown

Through this unthinkable sacrifice that He used to prove
That He is real every day and will be with us through each and every move

Yes, I took the Gift . . .
And, I have the Life . . .

Influenced

We are influenced by whatever fills our minds
And unfortunately much in society of all the wrong kinds

We spend endless hours reading all about celebrities each and every problem
Instead of opening our Bible and learning more about Him

We should meditate on His unfailing love . . . Psalm 48:9
That we can never get enough of

When was the last time we memorized a scripture
That was so beautiful, so relevant, and so pure

Again, whatever fills our minds in a day will influence us
in either a good or bad way

We can either find the purpose our lives are to play
or allow the sin of society to lead us astray

All God wants us to really do is love Him above all else
As we fall in love with Him and our heart melts

Then we will begin to understand what this fragile short life is about
About the promise of an eternal life without any doubt

And once we have the ultimate gift of salvation,
we will want the same for each and every person
As through our new lives we can influence another before our lives here are done

So today will you be a Christ-like influence or be influenced by the sins in a day?
It is up to us because of our choice some just may

Come to know Christ as their personal Savior because they were influenced

Influenced by you or me . . .
And now will have eternal life, you see
Oh, how beautiful our influence can truly be . . .

Just Like You

How I long to be just like You
With noble character, wisdom, understanding ~ a life of very few

For when you are with someone long enough
You pick up traits ~ some bad, some good, and all sorts of stuff

The exception comes when we become intimate with our Father above
We desire and strive to resemble all the qualities He consists of

We ask Him to mold us into what He wants us to become
Just like we shape our own child in a way
hopefully pleasing to God and then some

Children become resistant to change and can even rebel
No wonder we fight back when our Father tries to show and tell

For we are His children with our own agenda in mind
However, He may have a totally different plan for our lives ~ one of a more
abundant kind

Being just like You is what I long for
However, daily sin consumes me and I stumble time after time
and will forevermore

But I have to believe the depths of my soul and heart
That You are pleased that I strive to be just like You
when at first my day will start

I may constantly fall on my face
But You pick me up and remind me that being with You
is in the most perfect place

And some days you help me really shine
As You reward my efforts to be just like You as I walk the line

Of qualities that others know do not come from sinful me
But that God is cheering me on and wants others to see

That we can all become just like You
Through baby steps and never giving up of a promise so true

For the promise comes when we live in heaven with you one day
You will take us by the hand and gladly say

"Thank you for striving to be just like Me
For this is your reward and I, just like you,
can't wait to spend eternity with Thee."

Keeping Up with the Joneses

We have all heard the saying: Keeping up with the Joneses
For a long time this phrase has been popular and widely known

We think we need the bigger house, the bigger diamond, or the fancier car
But unfortunately there is always someone out there
who can still out do us by far

Then the disappointment settles in and now we want even more
Instead of stopping for a moment to consider what is this
Keeping up with Joneses really for?

It is due, my friend, to an emptiness felt inside
Instead of having Christ so abundantly within us reside

The thing I do like about Jones is it starts with the letter J
So turn Jones into Jesus and then you will be on your way

For you will finally find fulfillment and true peace
And at first when others hear of your new life they may talk and tease

But living for Jesus Christ has never been the more popular thing
However, the want for more stuff will slowly go away
in exchange for all that Jesus will bring

It is far greater than any gold or silver
And things that you never once considered will God begin in your heart to stir

Like helping someone in need
By finally noticing you can now have the opportunity
for one more struggling life to feed

The way you look at everything in your life from this day forward
Will make your past life of being so materialistic, so shamefully backward

All of a sudden, your so-called friends will become jealous of you
For somehow you found the most priceless gift now giving you life anew

You will no longer fit the norm
But now you have Christ to get you through each and every storm

Instead of turning to pills and alcohol
Now on Jesus Christ every time you can call

And He will guide you through life and give you
the most complete joy and satisfaction
As you stand on firm ground with so much traction

Does it sound too good to be true?
Well, just test Jesus and see all that He can do

He wants to fulfill the purpose for your life and mine
So we can, from this day forward, so compassionately shine

See, my friend, I know exactly what I am talking about for this used to be me
For I used to be quite materialistic
and could not wait to decorate the next room so lovely

So stop today Keeping up with the Joneses
And instead let us turn it around
To the best One who can ever be found

So today I choose, instead, to start Keeping up with Jesus . . .

Man of Few Words . . .

I may be a man of few words, but inside my heart, I can never quit expressing
how much I truly love you
Actions speak louder than words and I hope my actions of love reflect my
constant love for you, too

God must be rewarding me for something I have done right
For this man of few words never forgets to pray this simple prayer at night:

*"God, thank You for allowing me to spend this day with the love of my life
And help my actions this day, from this man of few words, speak volumes of
devoted love that I have for my beautiful wife . . ."*

Miscarriage

*This is a word that has become far too common today
A word that hurts so deep as if a part of me has gone astray*

*But I know, "Just as a Mother comforts her child,
so will I comfort you" Isaiah 66:13
Is a promise from God that abundantly becomes true*

*Another promise that I have been given
Is if I accept Christ as my personal Savior as I am living*

*The amazing reunion will occur
In heaven one day while on earth I find a way to endure*

*What better place for my baby to be
In the care and arms of my amazing Father taking care of thee . . .*

*From the depths of the word miscarriage is the word care
And even though some days it seems so unfair*

*Oh God help me to be an encouragement to other women
going through the same grief
As they begin to feel your comfort and mostly your love that brings so much relief*

*And "Thank You, Father, for taking care of each and every precious baby
for one day in Your perfect time we will reunite, but until then this baby will
remain such a strong part of me."*

*Who knows, maybe You wanted to protect them
from this cruel world of so much sin
so "Thank You again, Father, for allowing these babies in . . ."
Because as your word promises in 1 Corinthians 2:9*

No eye has seen
No ear has heard
No mind can conceive
What God has in store for those who love Him

Oh what a magnificent promise I will cherish in my heart as I persevere
And for your way of drawing me closer to You while you comfort me and say,
"You will be okay, my child, so dear . . ."

Written as my family and I suffered three
consecutive miscarriages after my son, Ethan.

To the many women who go through this difficult healing process, may God show you that He still loves you and has a perfect plan for your life. Never give up on having a child, but always be open to the possibilities of how He majestically will send you the perfect child He has for you. Do not try to help Him; just lay it at His feet and let Him do the rest. Your child will be worth the wait! My miracle baby Mia Faith was definitely worth the wait! And I realize now, I am doubly blessed, for I have two beautiful children on earth and three beautiful children I will meet in heaven one day. WOW!

Moments

It has been said, "We do not remember days; we remember moments."
These surely must be heaven sent . . .

For God only wants His best for His child
To give us those "WOW" moments and never anything simply mild

May God grant me more wonderful moments so true
For He allowed my most wonderful moments to be spent with you . . .

My Comfort Zone

*Being with you and still being in love is my favorite comfort zone
For we share everything as a couple as we have together grown*

*You are like all my favorite things
For being with you ~ a smile to my heart and face you constantly bring*

*Thank You, God, for my comfort zone through my true love
And may we find ways to step outside our comfort zone together as
we share all the mighty and mysterious ways You consist of . . .*

*"But he was pierced for our transgressions, he was crushed for our iniquities;
the punishment that brought us peace was upon him,
and by his wounds we are healed" Isaiah 53:5.*

Nail- Pierced Hands and Feet

*In our busy daily lives, we become so rushed and in a hurry
That we may accidentally stump our toe or slam our finger in a door, leaving us
with an intense throbbing ~full of pain and worry*

*One day when this happened to me
God used this as a mere reminder for me to grasp a little more clearly*

*How intense the suffering with pain that most of us could never even bare
When huge nails were hammered and pierced into Jesus' hands and feet
without any remorse or care*

*He must have agonized so deep as he lost so much blood
in this enormous cruel act
And this, my friend, is not make-believe, but biblical truth and fact*

And yet, Jesus, in all this suffering He did
Did this to save unworthy you and me, as through His brutal death on the cross
~every sin of ours was rid

And yet we seldom grasp the reality of this extreme act of love
when He suffered for you and me
Yet, this should be an eye-opening reminder of love
we could never really comprehend fully

He had nail-pierced hands and feet as He hung on a cross to die as He pleaded,
"My God, my God, have you forsaken me?" Matthew 27:46
For how much more pain would He have to endure, for each step of suffering
became more intense
And even more brutally?

My friend, will you embrace, today, the love the Father above has for you?
And accept His free gift of salvation given through His brutal death on a cross
so you can live a life in eternity as you meet your Savior and say,
"Dear Jesus, thank You . . ."

Never Enough

A Greek philosopher once said:
"To whom little is not enough,
Then nothing is ever enough."

Oh how true in a society of greed and wealth
When we should be more thankful for our families and health

Why do we constantly work ourselves as if a future of wealth is guaranteed
Instead of taking more time in a day to do at least one good deed?

We have accepted a mentality that it is never enough
While we work and work to get more and more stuff

If we would just invest the same amount of time
in the work God would have for us to do
Then maybe there would not be so much violence and destruction to live through

The only thing we should ever say "never enough" to
Is living for Christ and finding new ways
to help lost and dying souls become saved with The promise of life anew . . .

When we are laid to rest in our grave one day
There is not one possession we can take, as they will all just fade away

So today do not live with a mentality of never enough
Instead have only this mentality about God because with Him,
and only Him alone, We can never have enough . . .

Never Too Late . . .

It is never too late to get things straight
And do not allow Satan to whisper instead, "Oh just wait."

The time is now and the day is today
To remind one another how much we love them in all we do and say

Actions definitely speak louder than words
And we can either speak actions full of love or actions
full of anger that in our hearts stir

More resentment or more gentleness
sprinkled with love toward a parent or a child
For actions never seem to be just a little mild

They are things we remember and things we hold on to
For we do not remember days, we remember moments and this is thankfully and
sometimes regretfully true

Remember when you were a little boy and you wanted to be just like your dad
Remind him of this, for in his quiet time
you are growing up and he feels lonely and sad

Remember when your little boy wouldn't leave you alone
and give you a moment's peace
For he wanted to always be near you and be just like you
even when you were covered in grease

Pride holds us back from doing the right thing
For it always wants to blame the other person instead between two bring

Peace and love and respect and all the wonderful things
pleasing to Christ as we live
Learning more of ourselves in love to give

Do not let it be ever too late
For I have a phone call to make as I get things straight . . .

Our Beautiful Home

God sure has blessed us with a beautiful home
A place all our own . . .

It is not beautiful because of all the materialistic stuff
But because God is in the center of this home and that is enough

He has blessed us far more than we deserve or need
With plenty of food and good company on which to feed

Our biggest wish for our beautiful home is
That all will know it is not really ours, but His

We hope that everyone who enters in
Will feel an "aroma of love" that abides within . . .
Our Beautiful Home

Our Five Senses

Oh how amazing our five senses can be
From the ability to taste, to smell, to touch, to hear, and to see

God, help me to see through Your eyes more
And realize a need and have more compassion for

Someone truly in need this day
And not allow this moment to pass away

God, help me to hear all the sweet sounds around me
As I was listening through Your ears and hear Your wisdom so sweetly

God, help me to touch someone with a hug or a kiss
In a gentle way through Your arms and lips so as not to miss

An opportunity to make someone feel loved at this moment in time
As if they achieved their most difficult mountain to climb

God, help me to smell the sweet aroma of each blessing that You,
and You alone, so abundantly bring
And smell a flower that I never took time for in the spring
As my sense of smell so suddenly clings

Onto Your holy sweetness You want my life to enjoy
Instead of this world's sinful ways that constantly annoy

God, help me to taste the love of Your words that You give to me
As I speak in a manner more pleasing to Thee

God, I am so blessed I have these five senses
that can change a life in the most unique way
As someone sees You living through me in the Five most magnificent arrays
Of ways that You, through me, can display
Showing that You are still so real today

As You bring new life in us through . . . our five senses

Our Tithe

What does giving of your tithe really mean?
Maybe for most or for some it may seem

A requirement given by God to me
To help the church survive daily

Well, maybe this is where the problem begins
When our thinking is exactly like this ~ yes, what a sin

Instead, pray for God to change your mind to think more in a new light
Not to say, "Okay, God only 10 percent,"
but view your money with a new sight

Say, "God, 100 percent of this is Yours so please help me to use it
in a way to glorify You"
As I begin to see all what I give can really do . . .

When we begin to see how much God has really entrusted in us
Then it becomes more joyful without a lot of fuss

I have to wonder the grief of this world with so much unemployment
Is a way that God may be trying to give a hint

"You have not handled your money wisely and in a very selfish way
So to get your attention, I had to take it all away."

Just try to begin trusting every penny to God this year
And completely allow God to steer

He will take us down roads we never even knew existed
And had I not allowed God to drive, I would have missed

And this "joy of giving" will become what you want to do
Because you remained faithful in giving, and now this is a part of you

God will give back as we give with one hand
While the blessings will be given back in both hands

So think of it as a new honor today
"God, You sure have trusted in me far greater
than I deserve and I want my life to display"

A life committed to thinking more like You would want me to
To give generously and without reservation
because all this money belongs to only you

"Yes, God, today I pray
I will never view money in the very same way."

Thank You for what You have given to me
And for opening my eyes so I may truly see

And this gift I give as my joyful thanks to You
And I can't wait to see all that our tithe can do . . .

Written by: Mary Wasson
Potter's Hand Poetry

"He will bring you quietness with His love.
He will delight in you with shouts of joy."
Zephaniah 3:17

Precious Paws

God gives us special friendships that brighten our days
For through these precious paws, love is given in so many ways

Through a wagging of a tail, licks on the cheek, or jumping up for joy when we
give a gentle pat or loving embrace
All simple ways our true companion shows quiet love as each step behind ours
these precious paws trace

Our dedicated companion, our pet, says so much
when we look into their eyes
For there is only truth and never any lies

God, thank You for blessing our lives with these precious paws
that are such a big part of our family
For our days are filled with such joy as these precious paws
leave footprints on our hearts daily . . .

Power of Prayer

There is incredible power in times filled with prayer
Which seems, unfortunately today, to be quite rare

Satan uses his deception anyway he can today
To keep us from talking to God in the most intimate way

See, the only thing that can defeat Satan each day
Is this power of prayer where God will have the last say

And God is the only power that can put Satan in his place
Through anything he tries to throw our way or anything ahead we may face

Do not just pray in the morning or at night
Pray all day allowing this power of prayer to help you fight the good fight

And God will reveal Himself through thoughts that you used to think were your
own and many other unique and mysterious ways
For we allow Him to reign as number one in this game of life that we play

Yes, take back the power through the power of prayer
For having Christ in your life ~
Nothing in this world can ever compare

Praise You Enough

Oh Father, forgive me for I feel I do not praise You enough
As You have blessed my life with an enchanted ride
giving me more and more stuff

I should praise You in the morning for the luxurious bed
You allowed me to sleep upon
With fancy pillows, a beautiful comforter with matching pillowcases, and sheets
which many times I tend to dwell on

I should praise You in the daytime for the gentle breeze, like Your perfectly timed
fan to give me some relief
From the hot summer day that can rob me of comfort and energy like a sun-
scorching thief

I should praise You in the nighttime for the labor
You allowed my hands and feet today to give
Instead of taking another day for granted that You gave to me to live

In all things morning, noon, and night we should give You more praise
And never be ashamed in praise to gratefully use our hands to raise

As we focus on all the extra things You do for us
For You do not owe us anything and You do it because

You love us more than we will ever know
And through your blessings ~ You definitely do show

Over and over in scripture You tell us not in a hinting way, but very specific
To praise You, praise You, and then praise You some more for You are so terrific

And I have to believe the more we brag on You
The more You must say, "Just wait, My child, and see all that I can and will do."

When I step back and think for a moment like a child
When treated with praise after praise, they light up,
respond quicker, and want to show
us all the good things they have compiled

As if to say, "You haven't seen anything yet"
And this must be how our Father feels, for He wants to only give us His best ~
never things that He would regret

But He wants us to appreciate the simplest of blessings He gives
And also He wants to, each and every moment, live

In our lives and develop a daily relationship of praise
And not just in the crisis-filled days or simply a one-week-long phase

He wants us to want Him to be involved in every aspect of our lives
And just watch the transformation, for with Christ in us we can from now on
forever survive

Do not be anxious about anything, but in everything, by prayer and petition,
with thanksgiving and praise
present your requests to God Philippians 4:6 . . . is a promise so true
And with this, it is a reminder that I do not praise You enough, but I will
strive to praise You a little more today than
I did yesterday and praise you a little more tomorrow than I did today so I can
appreciate and love more and more of You . . .

Reflection in the Mirror

Before when I looked into the mirror to see if I looked okay
I would focus on my hair, my makeup, my wrinkles, oh yes, a few more to display

It was always a selfish time indeed
And never taking the time to truly read

Read deeper inside to a true reflection of the selfish me
Is it truly all about what others from the outside will see?

Or should I focus deeper on the inside for a reflection of Christ living through me
To see love, gentleness, compassion, warmth, empathy, patience,
and quality after quality that I should strive to be

For see, we will either like or dislike the reflection in the mirror
Because we either focus on every outward look that will one day disappoint or
focus on a Christ-like inward look that is more attractive, for sure

We can become so disappointed with the outward look as we view what we see
For charm is deceptive and beauty is fleeting yet a woman who fears the Lord
is to be praised Proverbs 31:30
Is a promise in your word so clearly

Oh how beautiful to look into a mirror and be transformed into an image of You
Oh God, I long for people to see You in me ~ so radiant a view

So as I see my reflection in the mirror in the days before me
Help me, Lord, to see Your radiant reflection shining all over,
for I cannot get enough of becoming more like Thee

Yes, I want to resemble Your most perfect look
For when I was born again, this is the new life I took

And each day I want to look more and more like You
A reflection so clear in the mirror
transforming into Christ through and through . . .

Rise and Shine

Rise and Shine . . .
Today is the day to not only rise, but Rise and Shine
For this day is mine all mine . . .

I can begin this day with the greatest attitude
As I feel refreshed and will begin today in a great mood

I can decide today to help someone in need
Not only with a kind word, but how about today also a good deed

Do something today that I would not normally do
Step outside my comfort zone and allow the Lord, through me, to shine through

Then as I relax in the evening to end my day
Allow God to speak to me and say,
"Thank you child for displaying Me in you today"

As I respond to Him, "God, I want to be more like You each day"
And not waste away another day . . .

So tomorrow I will again Rise and Shine
For with Christ shining through me this day is no longer mine all mine
See, it is a day given to me where I will allow God, through me, today to shine . . .

For it is a choice we make and each decision will determine our destiny
For me, I know what this has to be

Live today as if it may be my last day on earth
And allow God to use me to give someone new birth

New birth in Christ alone because He, too, DID Rise and Shine
And gave me the perfect gift of eternal life and said,
"Forever, this child is Mine all Mine . . ."

Sacrifice of a Soldier

There are so many sacrifices of a soldier
In hopes to give our great nation a better future

Sacrifice of leaving a wife who is expecting a child yet unborn
When the departure of choosing between family and country
leaves this soldier so torn

Sacrifice of not seeing all the first things that little children do
Only through advanced technology of video cams
captured to see a glimpse or a very small view

Sacrifice of missing a family member's birthday
When being together with family is a cherished time for their love toward each
other they can truthfully display

Sacrifice of celebrations like the Fourth of July
As families long to be with soldiers and soldiers long to be with families, as we
watch beautiful fireworks from the same starlit sky

Sacrifice of risking your life every day that you wake
To preserve our "One Nation Under God" and all mankind's sake

Sacrifice of losing a dear friend on the battlefield
As you talk to Jesus with grief and anguish, as you are humbly kneeled

Sacrifice of a physical injury that may never heal or just go away
But a constant reminder of a love for your country
as you go about your usual day

Sacrifice of mental anguish and nightmares that are still real
For it is a pain deep within that you will always feel

To every sacrifice our brave soldiers make
May we do our part and give back as prayer after prayer for each and every one
of them to God we take

And He will bless you, Soldier, for He sees all that you have done and will do
For protecting our great nation with glory and honor
is a privilege He chose to give to you

As Jesus made the ultimate sacrifice and died on a cross
to save us from all our sin
You are showing your own sacrifice of love for your country as you risk your life
for those you may never meet because your love resides,
from you brave Soldier, deep within . . .

Secret Ingredient

Once there was a man who watched his wife each time she cooked
Gently, pull down from the cupboard a box and take out a pinch and sprinkle it
onto the food of a secret ingredient as he would curiously look

One day his curiosity got the best of him so went she left to go to town
He pulled down this box for now it was time to wipe away this curiosity frown

Much to his surprise when he opened the box, he found that it was empty
He turned the box upside down and found the word Love written so gently
For this was the secret ingredient sprinkled in every preparation of food, you see

As Christians, we, too, have this secret ingredient, but the only problem is that
we want to keep it a secret
But God says, "Go into all the world and preach the good news"
as your fire for Him is constantly lit

Spread this secret ingredient of love for everyone you meet
So they can long to have your secret ingredient of this love that tastes
~ oh, so sweet . . .

Shine Through

This could be your time to Shine Through
Come on; don't be afraid to let others see the real you

To glow and glisten like a rare gem
Especially when we take the time to praise Him

Shine like a diamond in the ruff
So don't act so tough
Today is the day to say "enough is enough"

Instead, work on showing more love
So people can really see what you are made of

We may think this opens me up for pain
Yet if we turn it around and think
This opens me up for so much to gain

Love can bring so much pleasure
A quality that is difficult to measure
One that God will allow us to treasure

Are you afraid someone may see a blemish or two?
Well, if people only care about this then they just don't have a clue

Beauty can shine through
With our insecurities staying in their place
Even if we have a few blemishes upon our face
Don't ever let this erase

Your moment to shine through
Because this could be your opportunity for someone to see the new you . . .

Song of an Ocean Wave

As you relax for a moment on the Gulf shore beach
You can learn so much from God's beauty as through the song of an ocean wave
He does teach

It is a beautiful melody of serene music for us to enjoy and embrace
As we rekindle memories of past days and possible dreams ahead
through our minds we carefully trace

The song of an ocean wave puts us to sleep
As if God is singing a beautiful lullaby through His magnificent nature
for us to keep

In the background, He allows the seagulls to add their own harmony
As they always sing on time in a perfect chirping key

He speaks with boldness in an ocean wave as a storm draws near
Yet still calm enough to keep away ongoing fear

There is so much beauty that surrounds us in the same way
As if God wants to remind us how close He really is ~ yes, yesterday and today

Thank You, Father, for the song You sang to me through Your ocean wave
And may I rekindle the song of an ocean wave as it is another beautiful
stepping stone of life I save . . .

Thank you, Gary, for allowing us to enjoy some relaxation at your beautiful beach home each year. Many poems have been inspired as I have sat on the beach or on the balcony with pen and paper in hand. The beach is a reminder of how majestic God's beauty all around us truly is!

Splendor of Gray

Oh the splendor of our hair shimmering with silver and gray
For so many earned each and every one through years of hard work
and a life they now portray

Seeing someone with a head full of gray hair
Many times we think of someone full of wisdom, strength,
with tenderness and care

A caring for life as they have experienced so many of life's ups and downs
And those portraying a sweet spirit have in Christ truly found

How beautiful life can truly be
When we go through life ~ Jesus and me

MARY D. WASSON

Some prematurely turn gray and others wait many years
before their gray hair appears
And as each one of our hairs are numbered so each one of our gray hairs
does God find so dear

In Proverbs 20:29 it says
"The glory of young men is their strength, gray hair the splendor of old"
For each gray hair gained, there is an amazing story to be told

In today's society we cover as many gray hairs as we can,
for many boxes of hair color are sold
For we are fearful of aging and gray hair we think will just make us look old

And it is true that through stress we can gain many more
But it is how we handle that stress and what we are made of down to the core

And hair color no matter what color you have or even artificially have today
What matters is the true color of our soul as so many colors ~ a massive array

For there are no gray areas with God, you see
It is black or white and worthless is a life full of gray areas without clarity

So be proud of the gray hair He gives to you
But live a life of true white ~ one so pure, so precious, and unfortunately so few

Yes, gray hair is the splendor of old
But no matter how old, tell your story of Christ when your story is told

For God will bless the life you live today
when you take the time to stand up and be bold
And as you tell each page of your life book,
your true love for Christ will unfold . . .

Stained-Glass Prison

Intricate colors and details of beautiful stained-glass windows
can be found in many big churches today
With hidden pictures of crosses or Jesus as they are magnificently displayed

So appealing to the eye and pleasing to the soul when you glance at them
from within or from a passerby
Especially when the beautiful sunlight pronounces the colors so bold
as if God spoke to the sun as it shined forth from the sky

Unfortunately, in many big churches today lie a vast group of people
held in this stained-glass prison
For they are afraid or unwilling to enter into the outside desperate world
of struggling sin

And shine forth like this same brilliant light that shines into their stained-glass
prison because this would cause them to be outside their comfort zone
Into lands, countries, or neighborhoods for this is far too uncomfortable,
called the unknown

God can never show us all the great things He has in store
If we remain comfortable and never walk through the unknown door

How mighty a transformation could take place in this world if we allowed God
to show up like He never has before
By stepping into the unknown door and allow God to show how great and
mighty He can be as He mercifully gives grace a little more

It is time for us to open the windows of our stained-glass prison inside
And allow God to break the chains and completely within us reside

Then you will become desperate to help souls accept Him before it is too late
For when they accept Christ as their personal Savior,
He will clean away their past sinful slate

And they will have the promise of an eternity in heaven ~ yes, forevermore
And it will be because you allowed God to break the chains as you escaped
from the stain-glassed prison and opened the unknown door

So, God, please help me make this new commitment to You
To leave the stained-glass prison and shine forth into this world so I can see
all that You brilliantly can and will do . . .

Step Aside

Father above, teach me more how to step aside
And allow You fully through me to reside;
As always within my heart you shall reside

So many times I want to jump ahead of you, Father, so please forgive me
Again, help me step aside and allow You to shine through so abundantly

Help me use the words that would only come from You
Words so sweet, graceful, yet strong with conviction and power
so others can see what You can do

I can be stubborn and many times I want to do it my way or else none
Yet, if I would only step aside and turn my stubbornness into stewardship then
many more souls could be won

As I do mission work in a foreign land
Help me trust You to be the solid rock on which I will forever stand

From now on I only want to do it Your way
For I have found my purpose in life as I enter each new day

So let me step aside for this very moment
And truly allow You to use me for Your glory,
for I am one that You have chosen and sent

And anytime or anything that may try to get in my way better also step aside
For there is a world that needs to see Jesus
and He has already been tested and tried

And He has already won the victory
Which is what He wants to offer you and me

Help me to step aside and step within a life transformed to be
Completely with a promise of eternity in heaven pleasing to Thee . . .

Stewardship

God will entrust us with the resources we can handle
Not too much, not too little, only ample

For God knows the discipline we can endure
When it comes to handling money, which can be a curse or a cure

If all of a sudden we are blessed beyond measure
I wonder for how many will money immediately become their treasure?

Will it all of a sudden become more about what I want for me?
Or will I finally have the opportunity to reach out and change the world so richly?

We can sit around and reason with God
about all we would do to help others in need
But again I wonder how quickly we would turn against God in greed

For most I think too much money would be a curse
As we would find more and more ways to keep as much in our purse

"Oh I must save for a rainy day," we would hear
Instead of realizing God will meet our every need when needed, my dear

Stewards have a responsibility
As we are managers of all the resources God has given
and not because of our own ability

When we can become good and faithful stewards of all that He gives
Not just some, but all He gives from now on as we live

It is amazing how all of sudden your cup will overflow
again and again so quickly
For this is how we react to the needs around us
instead of contemplating them so slowly

The eagerness to thank God for your overwhelming resources
Instead of having Him tug at your heart or due to a guiltiness we meekly force

A financial gift given with reservation
Is one that may as well be kept because it is not given with satisfaction

Owners in this world have rights
Stewards have responsibilities and can make the decision to do what is right

Each and every time we are given resources through a hard-earned paycheck, a
gift, or an inheritance
Seek God first in each and every circumstance

For see it all belongs to Him and He doesn't need one penny we get
But He blesses our thinking when we with each penny never forget

That each and every blessing whether financial or any other kind
Can be used to glorify God and then the overwhelming joy we find

Makes giving a new part of the life we share
For we are becoming more like Jesus as we constantly care

And God has to be so pleased with His servant as He speaks,
"Well done, My good and faithful servant, for in your life you did humbly seek

And for this your stewardship has led so many people to Me; therefore, enter into
heaven so you can live
eternally with them, with Me, your Heavenly Father, and now come for I have
all these rich blessings to give thee . . ."

Strongholds

God, help me with this stronghold that gets the best of me
Whether an occasional drink, dabbling in drugs, sexual thoughts, or this
excessive weight that gets to be

Ways that keep me from drawing closer to you
As Satan tricks me into thinking, "Well, you can't be perfect and He will forgive
you because that is what He will always do."

As long as I allow these strongholds to stay as a permanent residence inside
Then it keeps me from being all that I can be for you
because I would rather escape and hide

Release this bondage and free these chains of darkness that dwell within
And instead, replace them with Your Holy Spirit to safely reside in

Help me to memorize scriptures from Your Holy Word
That I can recite back to Satan when he whispers his lies
that he makes sure I carefully heard

Then I can rebuke him and make him flee
For this is a promise in Your Holy Word given to me

Stronghold, you will be gone from my life as I never look back
Because I have a race with God and only with God
I will forever now stay on track . . .

Sympathy Prayer

Today, Father, this is my sympathy prayer
That even though I don't understand the precious loss
and I may even feel in my sorrow ~ how unfair

I know in my soul that each life is numbered in Your book
And some may feel too soon the life You took

Far sooner then we could have ever imagined
As they were not finished with all they would like to have done

This is where the wake-up call will begin
For some, they may never have the opportunity to do that one more thing again

None of us ever have that guarantee
For only You know how long our lives will be

So my sympathy prayer deep in my heart and soul
Is for others before it is too late to have the one guarantee if they know

You, Father above, so in eternity they, with You, will forever spend
And for this we will never question, "Why did this precious life have to end?"

The Apartment

A young married couple begins their life
as they rent their first apartment together
Knowing this is a temporary home, but excited as they are newly in love,
which they hope will last forever

Their one-bedroom apartment is a dream come true
Small, yet filled with lots of love ~ perfect for these two

A similar one bedroom apartment across the hall
holds a different meaning for a lonely man sitting inside
As he tearfully rekindles the mistakes in his life
and how he time and time again lied

He later drives by what would seem to be a mansion in most people's eyes
With a for sale sign in the front yard of this five thousand square feet home,
as he slowly drives by

This mansion was a dream-come-true home
With a wife and three children all his very own

Until stress from the corporate world got the best of him
Followed by long nights out with alcohol and women
leaving him feeling so empty and grim

He lost everything he had worked so hard for
And now his mansion is a one-bedroom apartment with a ragged front door

The apartment can hold so many meanings depending on where in life you are
Whether a young in-love married couple or a newly divorced lonely single man ~
for with either, God is never far

Sometimes everything in our lives is going so great
we just do not have time for God today
Or we are so far down in our pit of grief
we don't know what to God we would even say

Wherever your apartment has you as you travel through life
God wants to be there to help you and guide you through each happy moment or
days that bring nothing, but more strife

The apartment can hold so many different emotions for each one of us
And whether we stay in a small one-bedroom apartment
or move to a mansion in Beverly Hills~
it is only God who we can ever in this precious life trust . . .

The Car

There once was a SUV that I wanted really bad
And I made up my mind this would be the one I would have

Yes, it was a luxury vehicle through and through which had not even come out
Which meant I would be one of the first to have it, as I went all around town
here and about

Well, I knew in my spirit I really should take this huge request
and vehicle purchase to God
But deep down I was afraid because I feared He would never give me
the accepting yes nod

Well, I made this mistake once before
With a brand-new, white Mercedes right off the showroom floor

So this time I really wanted to trust Him through prayer
So I took this petition, like all others, to Him in humbleness without any flare

I asked Him to take this desire from my heart if it was not His will
As I waited for an answer with a spirit willing to hear, patient, and still

Well, all of a sudden I found out I would have to be on a waiting list for this
SUV and wait for days
Because there was such a great demand for this SUV, which later I found out
was just a phase

So slowly this began to turn me off
And then God used my husband to plant a new seed, oh so soft

He mentioned a popular SUV that had been redesigned
And for me to take a look and see if I like this kind

Well, immediately I became so excited because it was very beautiful, more
practical, and still sleek
So now I prayed about this much less expensive SUV
many times to God I did seek

A gentle yes nod would be great so I would know I could not go wrong
Little did I know this time I would keep it fairly long

In years before, I had to get a new vehicle every three years
As it was used as a company vehicle with a nice car allowance,
so never was there any fear

Well, we purchased the vehicle, for I received the yes nod
through complete peace I felt inside
And do not get me wrong for it is still the most luxurious ride

And I know I am very blessed as others may never in their wildest dreams
have a new car
So I try to not take this for granted, as God is way too good to me by far

A few months passed and I was listening to CNN one morn
And this SUV, the one I at first so desperately wanted, was announced live on
TV that its great reputation was torn

For it forcefully announced it was not safe at all
And consumers should not purchase it, as this entire SUV should be recalled

Immediately, I felt God speak, "See, Mary, I was protecting thee"
And I smiled and thanked Him because once again "He never fails me"

And today I absolutely enjoy my SUV even more
For I lost my career, too, and this must have been what God had in store

As He still blessed me with a beautiful vehicle that now will put miles on
for His work in the days ahead
And He will allow me to show up in style, I guess, not too fancy,
but with His perfect blessing instead

And I just have to sit back and wonder why
I ever question, for He sees the bigger picture; if only I would allow Him,
and not myself try

To believe He really needs my help in these big decisions from day to day
But know instead He works in mysterious ways

So thank You, Father, for this lesson from The Car
And thank You again for coming through for me like the most radiant
magnificent star . . .

The Closet

Months and years before a dream house is complete
Hopes arise that it doesn't lack anything, as this is to be your dream retreat

Stressful days consume you for you want everything to be just right
And today women want to certainly out-do each other so they find
elaborate ways to make even the closet perfect to the sight

The bigger the better lined in cedar and an added vanity for the extra touch
Again the goal is to out-do one another so there can never be too much

Then the reality sets in and now the focus becomes shifted
And now the concentration becomes making sure the closet is completely full
like a face lifted

For you cannot show off a well-to-do closet
without sinfully having it full from end to end
Or showing off would not be complete ~ oh, what a sin!

If we would ever focus this hard on loving our amazing God above
Then the selfish desire, which will never make you happy, could be replaced
with the most indescribable love

It would seem so different if your goal was to make the closet the most
elaborate place
For this is where you want to welcome your Heavenly Father during your
valuable quiet times in this dedicated space

Then it might make sense that you would only want the best
And, therefore, it has to be special and different from the rest

Society has poisoned us into thinking it is never enough
Like if we died tomorrow someone would actually care to close our casket full of
everything in the closet for, see, it is just that ~ stuff!

And it is stuff that we can never take with us
Instead, it will be left behind for all to cause a big fuss

It is time for us to care less and less about materialistic things
For they are a trick by the devil for us to avoid the ultimate ~ God the King!

Step back and look inside, my friend
To see the closet that you reside within

It is not too late to change your focus and fall in love with the Savior
And spend your remaining days in a new closet ~
The Closet of a personal relationship
with Jesus, making Him no longer a stranger . . .

The Cookies

Based on the message, "Judging Others", by Adrian Rogers

Once a lady was in the airport ready to catch her flight
But knowing the flight would be long she decided to pick up a little bite

So she bought some discounted cookies and some tea
And sat down in a little café beside a man sitting very closely

She proceeded to open the box of cookies and took one out
And then the man took a cookie, too, very confidently without any doubts

She became infuriated, but continued to keep her cool
Thinking to herself as he got another cookie, Can you believe this fool?

She sipped her tea and ate another cookie as she bit her tongue
to refrain from saying a nasty word
For if she started to lash out the entire airport probably would have heard

She would get another cookie and then the man would take one too
Until it came down to one cookie left, so now what would they do?

Well, the man beat her to it and broke the cookie in half
And ate his half of the cookie and left her the other half, and now all she could
do was sarcastically laugh

Finally it came time to board her flight
She picked up her things and headed to the plane with a fuming look of anger
showing on her face to let him know
what took place here was not all right

As she boarded the plane, she decided to get her magazine out of her bag
And inside her bag lay her box of unopened cookies with the discounted price tag

A feeling of embarrassment and remorse came over her
For she allowed, in her judging moment, so much anger in her heart to stir

And here was this man who was so gracious to share his box of cookies
in her mistake
And even left half of the last cookie for her to take

So be careful before we judge
Because so many times, for no reason, we hold a grudge

And what if Jesus held a grudge toward you or me?
We would do our best to avoid Him as we would flee constantly

But instead He doesn't judge us by being angry
He judges us the only way He can ~ so lovingly

So learn this lesson today
And judge not so you will not be judged in the same way . . . Matthew 7: 1–2

Leave the judging for Jesus to do
And just be thankful for His forgiveness so abundantly seasoned with His mercy
for me and you . . .

The First Step

The day a baby becomes anxious and brave enough to take his or her first step
Is one of those priceless moments you never want to ever forget

New chapters in these young lives begin from taking the first step
on that special day
For now a new independence occurs as they go on their way

Taking the first step on asking that beautiful young lady for a date
Because who knows; this just might be your perfect mate

The first step to walk into an interview that could land a career
Which would have never happened if you stayed back in fear

The first step into the cancer treatment center for chemo that you thought would
never happen to me
Is just a reminder of how delicate and precious life can truly be

There are so many first step moments that will happen in our lives
And we never have to go it alone if Christ is with us
to get us through each one as we strive

The most important first step we will ever make
Is accepting Christ into our hearts as this is the most important first step to take

And moments in life whether happy or sad
Can now reveal so much more meaning for us than they once had

For God has a purpose for your life and mine
When we allow the Holy Spirit to live in us and for Christ we then can shine

I wonder how many lives have never taken that first step
But instead are still crawling through life without any depth

You can go from walking to running through life with complete joy
As you want the whole world to know about Jesus
like a little child with their favorite toy

We just can't get enough of you Jesus as we daily live
And I want each step to count from now on
and each wrongful past step you forgive

Yes, I want to take the first step today
And I can't move unless You carry me from now on every step of the way

I yield my life to You, oh Lord, who allowed this first step to happen
And I am ready for each new first step,
for I want a life pleasing to You and not men

So let us begin this new chapter
For I have taken the most important first step that will ever matter . . .

The Graduate

I never thought this day would ever come
A little too fast it seems or a little too slow for some

But now the day has finally arrived for me to graduate
And I step back for a moment wondering my upcoming fate

Decisions like going to college or landing a new career
Decision after decision that can bring uncertainty and fear

Well, the best advice I ever did receive
Is the advice that I have a Heavenly Father who will never leave

He will help me make the tough decisions that lie ahead of me
As long as I ask Him to come along and help me see the foggy things more clearly

I was just so anxious to become independent and grow up so fast
Now the reality of becoming a failure or becoming a success is upon me at last

And no I am not as cool as I really thought before
Since I do not want to go alone, I ask You, Father,
to show me what You have in store

If I remember to bow my knees and ask You to guide me every step of the way
And realize from now on You must have a more important part to play

For in my failures You will lift me up
And in my successes You will overfill my cup

In Your scripture You promise, "For I know the plans I have for you,
plans to prosper not to harm you, plans to give you a hope and a future"
Jeremiah 29:11–12
As long as I remember to take this promise with me ~
only the best will come for sure

Mom and Dad, I am not your little baby anymore
Admittedly though, there are times
I still want to curl up in your lap just once more

I have to also remember ~ when you stumble, make it part of the dance
For I WILL stumble and God is always ready to give me another chance

So as I become the graduate
I am ready to begin this new journey foot by foot

And hand in hand
With God, for I realize He is the most important part
and with Him I now can . . .

The Porch

Many first moments can happen on the porch
Like a first kiss from that special date as they light your love torch

Permission from a father to take his daughter as your wife
As together this special couple will begin a new life

Family get-togethers as grills are lit
Enjoying the simple American foods like hamburgers and hot dogs
as family and friends sit

Visit with elders like we did back when
You could just drop by for a visit and even allow strangers in

Protection from a heavy rainstorm that may come around
As we listen from the porch and hear the falling rain sound

The place where handshakes were given as the deal was sealed
As we humbly fell to our knees and thanked God as we kneeled

The place where we relax and take it all in
As we erase bad memories from our day and embrace good memories
that reside within

The porch can hold so much that can happen in our lives
Whether the smell-of-fresh-paint new one o
r a weathered-distressed-wood-look old one ~
the porch can always survive

So what does your porch hold?
As on your own porch of life your story can carefully be told

Yes, memories I will cherish from the porch today
For stories of love and laughter, and of years and tears, will within my heart,
because of the porch, forever stay . . .

The Surgeon

How incredible to one day become The Surgeon
Where a life so fragile can be placed in your hands solely depending upon

Each delicate move that you make
And sometimes very risky decisions you decide to take

Well, my friend, as Christians we are our own success stories
with a new life in Christ we partake
Becoming The Surgeon for Christ because for many lost souls
it is life or death at stake

Sometimes we almost dread going into surgery for in this very moment
we become bold witnesses as we share the good news of Christ and His love
Afraid of what others may think or say, for we feel so inadequate and many
times so unworthy of

We should strive to become one of the TOP Surgeons in the country
And it does not happen overnight, as it takes years and years
for others to finally see

The Surgeon that everyone comes to, for they see all that you have done for this
Jesus you love so much
Therefore, they want to feel Jesus, too, through your surgeon hands of
God's amazing touch

So any and every time you have the opportunity to practice your surgeon skills
Just remember the brutal death of Jesus on the cross
and strive to be a bold witness with all your courage and will

Let us ALL be The TOP Surgeon in our field
Of winning lost souls for You, dear Lord, with an abundance of Your amazing
grace on which to build . . .

The Sweet South

So many wonderful things happen in the sweet South
With priceless Southern accents and those who like to talk, as they must like to
hear words spoken from their mouths

Where "Thou shalt love thy neighbor" can come quite easy for many
As sharing and caring is known if you have little or plenty

Calling people "honey" or "sugar" is a compliment
As it is a gesture of being comfortable with someone and it is a sweet sentiment

Pulling over on the side of the road so someone can pass you by
As you enjoy a Sunday ride with your family for in the sweet South we spend
time together without a special reason why

Knowing someone will lend a helping hand to a stranger who has a car flat
While you visit about where you are from and this and that

Always having a dessert like fresh apple pie with a pot of coffee for company
who decided to stay for awhile
For in the sweet South, it is always about going the extra mile

Fixing up an old truck and making it like new
For these truck classics today are too few

Going to church every time the doors are open
For fellowship with other believers is wonderful whether a hundred or ten

Taking extra time to visit those who are sick and need a friend
For compassion must have originated in the South as a helping hand
many will always lend

Sharing fresh fruits and vegetables from your garden
when the harvest is in bloom
Until you have a freezer full without a lot of room

Where you can always fish and hunt with rare excessive cold days
Which makes it far more enjoyable most would say

Farming is a way of life for many in the South through the year
For from their beautiful harvest many crops are produced and sold,
so plentiful and dear

Screened-in porches are a great way to relax any time of the day
Or a screen door is like an open door policy for those to come in and stay

Always having sweet iced tea as the beverage of choice everywhere you go
For in the Sweet South ~ sweetness is ours to bestow

Yes, I feel so blessed to be from where I call home ~ The Sweet South
And may I give thanks to my Father above as I compliment all of its sweetness
from my mouth . . .

The Waiting Room

So many thoughts can enter your mind as you patiently wait in the waiting room
Whether good news that can bring relief or bad news
that can bring unforeseen doom and gloom
And the "what if" question captivates your thoughts as you continue to assume

Patients bring crossword puzzles or books to read to divert their attention
For if they sat there too long, it would leave room for much apprehension

This may be the perfect time and place to quietly bring your cares to the Lord
as you wait
For there is no better time and it is definitely never too late

News like hearing that you indeed have cancer
And no one can seem to give much hope or the correct answer

News that your baby has gone on to be with the Lord in heaven now
As you play back in your mind
What did I do wrong to cause this miscarriage somehow?

News that your family member in ICU is fading fast
Therefore; you may want to be by their side as they peacefully pass

News that you will need the surgery you put off for so long
For instead of getting better as you had hoped, it is all going wrong

Today as many wait patiently in the waiting rooms
This is where a new hope inside of us can blossom and bloom

For no matter what comes our way today
God can use our story to glorify Him in the most magnificent way

See, there is someone else sitting in the waiting room somewhere
Waiting to hear some good news or bad news and making many feel, today, that
life is somehow unfair

And we could be the inspiration that they need
As we share Jesus through our testimony-planted seed

For we are never alone as we wait in the waiting room
As Jesus is right beside us wanting to give us His plans for a hope and a future
instead of all the negativity we assume

So I want to make room for You, Jesus, as I wait
For in the waiting room, being together, is pleasant and peaceful as I share it all
with You, my soul mate . . .

Time for a Nap

Every Sunday after church it is so refreshing to make time for a nap
Just like a new baby lying for the first time in her mommy's lap

I believe God created us to relax and take time for a nap every now and then
So as to renew our minds so we can continue on with our day again

He created nap time for mommies and babies
As a way to give moms a little break and keep her sanity maybe

Some days we hold so much in our minds
And you may think taking time for a nap will "Put me so behind,"

But maybe, just maybe, time for a nap will allow God
to put a little dream in our path
For in His mysterious ways He hath

Revealed another purpose He wants us to fulfill
Allowing this world to see today how He is still real

Next time you think of making time for a nap
Just think; this may be refreshing, renewing, and maybe,
just maybe, revealing perhaps . . .

Time for Me to Go . . .

My child, it was time for me to go . . .
But one of my final prayers was that God would let you know

I had the privilege of being a mother to you
A legacy you have passed on and God and I are so thankful, too

For so many years you brought more joy than words could ever express
Knowing I never deserved you for a daughter, nonetheless

I, as so many mothers, never wanted to become a burden
So God in His perfect time allowed His angels from heaven to descend

And take me to a place where no suffering will ever occur
Only reunions and rejoicing with a new body of perfection and holiness ~
one that will endure

For all of us must die one day
And all that matters is our new lives anyway

For our lives on earth are like a speck in time, for some too soon
and others awhile before it will go away
And the reality is an eternity in heaven for some or an eternity in hell
for others ~ absolutely no other way

Daughter, I had so many good memories during my time on earth with you
But God wants you to know now it was time for me to go . . .
For
No eye has seen
No ear has heard
No mind can conceive what God has in store for those who love Him . . .
1 Corinthians 2:9
And Christ and I have much new living to do . . .

Two Become One

Little girls dream of becoming a princess and live in a castle
or a bride on their wedding day
Dressed so beautifully, so for most, including the groom ~
she will take their breath away

All the months of preparing has finally come to an end
And today, two become one as their new lives together will ascend

This moment has finally arrived for this couple and their families
As they make their vows and pray to God to bless this couple in unity

Finally, they will become man and wife as the presentation is made
"May I present to you Mr. and Mrs." ~ this sentimental moment,
we hope will never fade

The celebration begins with lots of food, family, and friends gathered to wish
this newly married couple farewell
As they rekindle stories of the wedding preparations
and decisions about the cake, as they laugh and tell

The cake with intricate details almost too delicate and beautiful to eat
Is finally cut as photos are taken and toasts to the bride and groom are made, as
everyone finally relaxes and takes a seat

At the end of this wonderful wedding celebration
The couple is sent off on their honeymoon as two become one ~
for husband and wife
begin their new life with so many wonderful anticipations

God bless Your children as Two Become One
And may You guide them through their new life with Your one and only Son

Yes, Two Became One . . .
And Husband and Wife, with this new chapter of life,
have just begun . . .

Trust

"Trust in the Lord with all your heart and lean not on your own understanding;
in all your ways acknowledge Him, and
He will make your paths straight" Proverbs 3:5–6.

If a complete stranger approaches us and asks us to do something
to help him this day
The immediate response would be, "What is it?" we would quickly,
without hesitation, say

The stranger replies, "Just trust me, please."
Most of us would walk away with a glance like, "you must think I am crazy" or
"you must have some disease."

The reason we would not gladly help this stranger in need
Is because we do not know him on an intimate or personal level; therefore, the
trust has not been built to help with any sort of deed

Now if someone we love so deep like a mother, a spouse,
or possibly even our child
Asks for help tomorrow not stating if the task would be heavy or mild

We may still ask in curiosity, "What do you want me to do?"
With a reply from our dear loved one, "Just trust me and tomorrow I
will clearly show you."

Due to this strong bond and love we have developed toward this loved one
We would still agree to help get their task done

This is exactly how it is with our Lord and Savior
When we begin to welcome Him into our hearts and homes with an open door

We begin to know Him as our love grows so deep
And then certain scriptures suddenly make sense and we can recite them and in
our hearts keep

"Delight yourself in the Lord and He will give you the desires of your heart"
Psalm 37:4.
For desires He has for you become desires you want for yourself because now He
is such a vital part

The goals you once set for yourself seem to fade away
As your focus remains on the love you have for your Father and your desire to
serve Him in your heart now stays

As this relationship of love builds in every aspect of life
We begin to see God's hand in every great thing that happens and even those
things that bring us strife

This becomes a total commitment as we acknowledge Him
in anything and everything
And this confidence of trust follows for we now know He only wants to bring

The very best for our lives as we clearly see the purpose He has for you and me
And it comes from "you have to know Him to love Him"
followed by ~ trust fully

What a glorious moment one day
When we take our Father's hand and hear, "Well done my good and faithful
servant" as we enter into heaven as another prized masterpiece of clay . . .

Two-Seated Bike

I used to go through life alone on my two-seated bike
Going anywhere I wanted and trying new things I thought I may like

So many times the two-seated bike would become front heavy
And I would come crashing down with cuts and scrapes because it was difficult
to keep this bike steady

When I accepted Christ as my personal Savior,
I could not wait to say, "Get on, Lord"
For now my ride would become more fun, as I had a new friend, Jesus,
to keep me company and not bored

Well, somewhere along the way Jesus said to me, "Mary, let us switch places"
As He moved to the front and I moved behind Him, for He wanted to guide me
down the right paths through all my different life phases

Sometimes I would become really scared as Jesus seemed to be going rather fast
Or He would begin to move up a steep mountain and say to me,
"Pedal harder, for your endurance has to last."

Some days we would enjoy all the beauty life had to offer
As we would enjoy long, peaceful, and serene rides with the gentle wind on our
backs, as this sure made pedaling much easier

*Along the way, I would want to hold on to the stuff in life
that I felt was so important to me
But Jesus said, "Give it away, for it will slow down our journey."*

*Many times, I would want to take the short cuts to get where we were going
Yet Jesus would take me the long way so I would see the bigger picture
He was showing*

*And I began to trust Him more and help Him less
For worry can drain the life from us, when in Jesus we should find complete
peace and rest. Luke 12:22–26*

*I am so excited to see where our two-seated bike will lead
And Jesus has never had any accidents, so I have the best leader, indeed*

*Maybe we will pass you along the path we tread
And I hope to wave to Jesus and you as Jesus and I move forward with my
ultimate life's purpose ahead . . .*

We Didn't Even Ask

*We are given the most perfect gift that anyone could ever receive
When we make the choice and in Christ believe*

*See Jesus died the most brutal death on a cross to save us from all sin
We didn't even ask for this kind of sacrifice,
much less this expression of love so deep within*

*Yet we ask for so many things today
And wonder if God hears us when we pray*

*My friend, we didn't even ask and again love
we could never comprehend or measure
Was given freely so we can enjoy life more abundantly with so much pleasure*

When we begin to put Christ first in all that we do
Most of our things we think we want will dwindle away to very few

For it is all about letting others know how honored we should all feel and be
For God loved us so much that He allowed His one and only Son as in doing so,
His Son made one last plea,

"Father, if you are willing, take this cup from me; yet not my will, but yours be
done" Luke 22:42
As God, because of love, allowed the sacrifice of death from His one and only Son

We didn't even ask and yet love like we will never know
From God, through His son Jesus, did show

Thank You, God, for showing us how magnificent Your love is
We didn't even ask and yet Your love did this . . .

What If . . .

Being a teacher every day can be tiresome and mundane
And some days to the undisciplined nature of a child ~
days where you could go insane

But What If in your class was a future president to lead this country
With an interview from you, Teacher, that had the privilege to teach this child so
dedicated and carefully?

Would you teach your class in a different way
Knowing that you could be an important part to play?

What If you had a student in your class today
who may discover an amazing invention one day
Would you feel like you helped this child to dream a bigger dream
before sending them on their way?

183

What If a child graduated from high school
Would you feel just as important, for in your class
you helped them learn the golden rule?

What If you had a child who seemed to be out of control
with very few manners just looking for attention
Would you treat this child with as much encouragement, knowing you could be
the only person who could truly give proper direction?

And every step of the way, pray to the Father above
to show you how to reach this child
Who may be to most, at first glance, too unruly to worry with
as their demeanor may be completely wild

Well, What If our Father above only wanted to know
the Successes and none of the obvious Failures?
We can humbly thank Him for wanting to know every failure
that He can turn into a success
one day with an amazing testimony and Christ-living adventure

Being a teacher may not earn the biggest pay
But the pension of shaping and touching lives
is one with rewards that will forever stay

So the next time you feel yourself getting into the same old routine and
wondering if you have made a difference to one this day
Just know the Father above will bless every word taught and every encouraging
word given when done with an attitude as if we are doing it for Him today

What If one day
The child you taught could repay

Through a life that was molded and shaped by you, Teacher
A doctor, a nurse, a farmer, a fireman, a soldier, a mother,
a father or a president with the
Father above as their main feature . . .

What Truly Matters . . .

There are moments in our lives that truly matter . . .
Like having a tea party with our young daughter because it means so much to her

Or how about throwing ball with a son so he can feel like an all-star
As he looks at his daddy like this same man looks at his favorite sports car

Taking time to be a kid again when we make a "play date" at the park
And play and play until finally it gets too dark

How about taking a vacation day during a work week because you want a
special "date day" just for you and your kid
For these seem like little things that will one day become so grand because you
didn't just talk about it, but you did . . .

I wonder how happy this makes God
As He must look upon us and gently smile with a pleasing nod

The more we take time for others around us
Is when I believe God will in us begin to trust

Trust us with some of His most precious things that only He can offer
Bringing us more days with peace, love, and laughter

When we begin to understand what truly matters in this delicate life that we live
Is when we just can't get enough of wanting to give

So I want to give time for someone today
Because this truly matters and no one can ever take that away

Minutes turn into hours, hours into days, days into months, and months into years
And I want each one to truly matter because each moment in time I spent with
God and above all else this is . . . What Truly Matters

What Would I Do?

What would I do if I didn't have a cell phone to make all my calls
Or all the fancy gadgets like iPods, chat rooms, or video cameras to install?

What would I do if I didn't have electricity for all the luxuries
I take for granted
Like TV, coffee makers, lights, air conditioners, and of course, refrigerators with
the assortment of foods on which I can be fed?

What would I do if I didn't have my car to take me all the places I wanted to go?
For this would just be unimaginable for most, you know

What would I do if I didn't have my warm home to keep me safe at night?
For no matter how my day went, at home everything seems to be all right

What would I do if I didn't have, for most,
a wide choice of clothes to clothe my back?
For a closet full of clothes ~ many today seldom lack

The most important question we all should ask today
What would I do if I didn't know Jesus as my personal Savior this very day?

The most important question that should ever come to our lips
Is one that we ignore as if we have a secret-guarantee-of-a-long-life tip

Yes, a tip that we will live so very long
When instead in a blink of an eye, we could simply be wrong

What would I do if I didn't know Jesus today and die?
Go straight to a damnation in hell, as my new life would be living in a pit of fire,
as the Bible never lies

My friend, know Jesus today before it is too late
And no matter how minor or major your past has been,
accept Jesus and get your life straight

What would I do if I didn't know Jesus ~ yes, really know Him in my heart?
I would stop right now and ask for forgiveness and fall to my knees as I ask Him
to give me this fresh start

And the most important question of all will now have an answer
As I am promised a new life full of perfection as I enter into heaven
and live forever after . . .

"When I"

So many times in our lives we say, "When I"
As if we have a guarantee of our days here on earth
without realizing they could just pass us by

Some live what seems a lifetime of old age
And others so young are gone before we get to see their next page

Pages of life in a book that was not yet complete
But who are we to say how our own lives should go
with mere perfection without defeat?

"When I"
"When I"
Take these words and stash them away
And replace them with words that we should constantly portray
"For now"
"For now"

"For now" my clock is ticking on this earth and I have so much to do
To make a difference in this world by demonstrating a little preview

Of the love You and only You can offer, my Father above
As You come into our hearts to live within us and help us show Your love

"For now" I have work to do with souls to win
For see, one day I want these souls, too, to enter in

"When I" is an excuse for the very lame
Instead, quit making every excuse for we have heard them all the same

"For now" I have the clear direction of the path I need to take
"For now" there is so much destruction and lives at stake

Life after life will go to heaven or hell
And this is biblical fact that we should not be afraid to tell

The only time I feel the urge to say "When I" is
"When I" survey the wondrous cross it gives me such despair and pain
To know Jesus loved me this much and died a brutal death to save us with an
eternal life in heaven to gain

How amazing at the end of our journey of life here
We can take our Father's hand in love with absolutely no reservation or fear

And hear Him say:
"When I came to heaven after my death on that cross, you see
I came to prepare a place for you
For now you will have eternal life with Me, For now and From now on so
abundantly . . ."

When Sometimes Enough is Enough

When sometimes we come to a point in our lives when enough is enough
And walking away is never easy; instead it is hurtful and rough

Yet, God helps us realize that you cannot help someone
who doesn't want the help, you see
Just like when God wants to help you or me

We fight it with all our might due to stubbornness, or we're afraid of the
changes we will have to make
When if we would allow God to work in our lives ~ there is no telling all the
places He would gently take

"For I know the plans I have for you, plans to give you a hope
and a future, not to harm you". Jeremiah 29:11
And this is a promise in His word written specifically for us,
as it is delivered so loving and so true

Another problem that seems to always arise
Is that dreadful pride that never dies

And we always think we can handle any and every thing that comes our way
When God uses obstacles in our lives for us to come to Him and say

"God, please help me make the right choices in this difficult situation I am in"
As He will comfort you with a peace and take over your challenges
as He resides within

Do not ever allow Satan to trick you into thinking that you cared a little less
Instead sometimes enough is enough and we have to walk away
as you pray to the Father to bless

This person you care so much about
And only want God's best for their life without any doubt

God will bless each prayer that you took the time to give on their behalf
As you recall better days with precious memories that still today make you laugh

My friend, it is understandable to have difficult people sometimes in our lives
As God can use these people as a gift to help us with patience and perseverance,
as in our lives we strive

Remember, everything bad can be turned around for good
and used by Almighty God
As He shapes our lives into what He wants us to become,
as we find our purpose and He gives
His pleasing nod

*Yes, sometimes enough is enough, but never when it comes t
o all that God consists of
As we always remember, God will never get tired of giving us more and more of
His perfect love . . .*

Wind Chime

*As you sit quietly and listen to the welcoming sound of a wind chime
It can take you back to precious moments in time*

*The gentle breeze that accompanies the wind chime causing it to move
Can be, oh so welcoming, as well, because joined together, they can be
quite soft and smooth*

*It is like a music box in the background
As you listen to all the soothing sounds*

*It can be like a dinner bell calling birds to eat
For bird watching makes these peaceful moments so complete*

*It is a reminder from God that He is always near
As He creates melodies so pleasant to the ear*

*The wind chime is never too loud ~ only soothing and serene
As all of God's majesty in the beauty of His nature is seen*

*Peaceful moments of magic happen through a wind chime
As cherished memories bring you back to precious moments in time . . .*

Your Time

As I eagerly await an answer from You
On a deep desire of a dream I want to come true

I realize I do not want to run off and leave You for I need You to be with me
Or I will keep looking back for You and stumble over and over, for the direction
ahead is unclear and scary

And then I realize I do not want to lag behind
And just be a talker without being a doer, for there are too many of this kind

Instead, if I can learn to go at Your pace
Then we will together make it to the most perfect place

For along the way I will fall or even trip and then stub my toe
And then You will pick me up, comfort me, carry me, and then off we will go

In Your time we can never go wrong
And the wait will never seem too short or too long

For in Your time Your peace will surpass all understanding
And it is a complete peace that doesn't just last for a day, but it is everlasting

So today, Father, I want to wait for Your time
As I listen to You gently speaking
like the most beautiful melody of a wind chime

Yes, thank You, Father, for showing me in my own life ~ it is all in Your time . . .

Psalm 37:23-24
As I wait on God to fulfill His perfect plan in my life

FATHER AND SON POEMS

These next series of poems were written for a father reading it about his son and then a son reading this about his father. Relationships in families can go through rough times and my hope is that God can use these words to help someone you love realize how fragile life is, and there is never any guarantee; you can make things right before it is too late. May God grip your heart through "The News Came Today."

These poems, "Becoming More Like Me," "Growing Up and Getting Out," "Never Too Late," and "The News Came Today", were written for a father and son, who were struggling with teenage vs. parent issues, as a way to help them realize just how precious each day in peace together can be, and that one day it may be too late if we continue to live in anger and disrespect. Hopefully, these poems can help someone in your life who is struggling with relationship issues.

Becoming More Like Me . . .

Seasons change and children grow
No more hanging out with Mom and Dad, for this is no longer cool, you know

Disrespect takes the place of respect in our home more these days
As Mom gets caught in the middle in more than just one way

Everyone tells my son he is becoming more like me
Does that mean good or bad qualities that others see?

Do I put God first in all that I do?
And if I don't, how can I expect my son to?

Do I lash out in anger with eyes that could kill?
Or does my son see the love in my eyes that I so deeply feel?

Do I like who I am when I look into the mirror?
Because God sees beyond the surface as He wants in my life to grow nearer

"It is never too late to become more like Me"
Words from our Heavenly Father that I long for others to see

So if I become more like Christ, then my son will too
For my son is a reflection of me and, through love,
many sacrifices we will make and do

How awesome to look into the mirror and see
Beyond me to my son, of whom I am so proud for who he has become,
because behind him I see a reflection clearly . . . of Thee

Growing Up and Getting Out . . .

I never thought this day would ever come
That I have now turned into a young adult and growing up
and getting out is quickly approaching
as I beat to a new drum

No more people telling me what I can and cannot do
For they just don't understand how I have changed
and what I have been through

Well, my friend, "Honor your mother and your father"
is a command from Almighty God
And growing up and getting out can lead you into temptation
as Satan gives his welcoming nod

For He will deceive you into thinking you know it all when you don't at all
And this is why God gave wisdom to your parents so in the good times as they
praise Him and in the bad times as they rebuke Satan
~ in both, as a family, they can stand tall

Respect in a home is something you earn
As you look to your family and allow them to teach as you carefully learn

Take it from someone who has walked in your shoes
I allowed Satan to deceive my life with alcohol, sex, and his lies as I felt so used

And I must have hurt God so much
Because I never deserved the wonderful parents He hand selected for me with
His gentle touch

As you, as I did, become really honest with yourself
and realize it is about selfishness
And right now growing up and getting out is all you think of, for deep down,
when it comes to others, you really could care less

Most likely your parents may have rebelled in some of the same ways
And they are praying to God right now
that Satan cannot get a hold of you and lead you astray

If your parents did not love you very much
then they would not care what you do
But simply, they love you and only want God's best for you

So step back for a moment and remember every sacrifice
through the years they made on your behalf
And as these memories you recall, together again, you can cry and then laugh

For you would never be where you are today
If it wasn't for your parents who loved you
with the love of Christ in their own special way

So let growing up and getting out take a back seat for awhile
For your mother and your father will not always be around and you can honor
them as God commands us to and allow God to look down from heaven
on your family and . . . smile

Never Too Late . . .

It is never too late to get things straight
And do not allow Satan to whisper instead, "Oh just wait."

The time is now and the day is today
To remind one another how much we love them in all we do and say

Actions definitely speak louder than words
And we can either speak actions full of love or actions
full of anger that in our hearts stir

More resentment or more gentleness
sprinkled with love toward a parent or a child
For actions never seem to be just a little mild

They are things we remember and things we hold on to
For we do not remember days, we remember moments and this is thankfully and
sometimes regretfully true

Remember when you were a little boy and you wanted to be just like your dad
Remind him of this, for in his quiet time
you are growing up and he feels lonely and sad

Remember when your little boy wouldn't leave you alone
and give you a moment's peace
For he wanted to always be near you and be just like you
even when you were covered in grease

Pride holds us back from doing the right thing
For it always wants to blame the other person instead between two bring

Peace and love and respect and all the wonderful things
pleasing to Christ as we live
Learning more of ourselves in love to give

Do not let it be ever too late
For I have a phone call to make as I get things straight . . .

The News Came Today . . . (For Son)

The worst phone call of my life came today
News that my father was killed in a car accident in such a tragic way

"No, it cannot end this way!"
As my father left in anger, we had another fight and I watched from the
window as he sped out of the driveway

Life should and cannot end like this
For we didn't get to make up to fill my memories with peace, love, and bliss

"God, this is just not fair;
After all we have been through
and how much I truly and deeply do love and care

I thought it was never too late
For us to get all our difficulties and silly fusses and fights all straight."

Why did I listen to Satan, as he once again lied
And persuaded me to keep blaming others,
as my true feelings I would bury and hide?

What if God gave me one more chance
To fix things and turn around some of my circumstances?

I would honor my mother and my father the way I should
God, with Your help each day, I feel I really could

What if the news came today and it was the worst news, you see?
Would you have any regrets or would you proudly stand up to give the eulogy?

Do not ever let it be too late;
Be the bigger person and allow God to guide you and do not ever wait

For one day your worst news could come or your best news could come
That your dad just called to say, "I love you, Son, and I just wanted you to know
how proud I am of what you have become . . ."

The News Came Today . . . (For Father)

The worst phone call of my life came today
News that my son was killed in a car accident in such a tragic way

"No, it cannot end this way!"
As my son left in anger, we had another fight and I watched from the window
as he sped out of the driveway

Life should and cannot end like this
For we didn't get to make up to fill my memories with peace, love, and bliss

"God, this is just not fair,
After all we have been through
and how much I truly and deeply do love and care

I thought it was never too late
For us to get all our difficulties and silly fusses and fights all straight."

Why did I listen to Satan, as he once again lied
And persuaded me to keep blaming others,
as my true feelings I would bury and hide?

What if God gave me one more chance
To fix things and turn around some of my circumstances?

I would treat my son the way I should
God, with Your help each day, I feel I really could

What if the news came today and it was the worst news, you see?
Would you have any regrets or would you proudly stand up to give the eulogy?

Do not ever let it be too late;
Be the bigger person and allow God to guide you and do not ever wait

For one day your worst news could come or your best news could come
That your son just called to say, "I love you, Dad,
and thanks for all you are helping me to become . . ."

CPSIA information can be obtained at www.ICGtesting.com
Printed in the USA
LVOW060907031212

309774LV00002B/11/P